Special Educational Needs *in practice*

REVISED EDITION

Edited by Selena Ledgerton

This book is dedicated to my beautiful son Jaycen who makes me beam and fills my heart with love and pride.

Illustrated by Cathy Hughes

Published by Practical Pre-School Books, A Division of MA Education, St Jude's Church, Dulwich Road, Herne Hill, London, SE24 0PB
Tel: 020 7501 6753 www.practicalpreschoolbooks.com

© 2010 MA Education

Special Educational in practice revised edition ISBN 978 1 907241 02 4

The role of the SENCO: an introduction

The updated Special Educational Needs Code of Practice sets a requirement for all early years settings, including approved childminding networks, to either employ a member of staff or train an existing one as special educational needs coordinator (SENCO). Whilst the organisation of this role may differ among settings, it is a mandatory and very important role with major implications for all areas of early years provision.

The overall responsibility of the SENCO is in monitoring and coordinating the implementation of the Code of Practice within the setting, so if you have just been employed or appointed as SENCO, what is expected of you and who can you turn to for advice? The following headings provide a summary of the areas you will need to give consideration to first of all.

The Code of Practice and policy for special educational needs

The first thing you will need to do is make sure you are familiar with both the Code of Practice (see page 70) and your setting's special educational needs policy.

The Code lays down a statutory obligation to ensure that an up-to-date SEN policy is implemented in the running of each group, and you will be responsible for overseeing the operation of this policy. Assuming this policy is

appropriate, you will need to make sure that all staff members are aware of the policy and what is expected of them, that it is being carried out and review progress.

You may need to organise a staff training session to explain the policy further and check understanding amongst the staff team. With support from the staff you work with, you will then be in a position to assess how the policy is actually being implemented.

Coordination of provision for children with special educational needs

Whilst staff working directly with individual children with special needs will be supporting them and observing and assessing their progress, you should support them in making assessments of need and ensure all known information is collected from a variety of sources. This may involve liaison with outside agencies, including those already involved with the child, and will always involve liaison with the parents. You will need to make sure that parents understand your involvement and arrange and review meetings with the child and everyone involved each term.

It is important that staff understand they are required to keep records of children's progress, noting concerns, and these will provide valuable information when you liaise with staff to produce Individual Education Plans (IEPs) and plan relevant provision for the child.

Support for individual children and their families

You will need to work closely with the child's early years worker and parents to decide upon the action to be taken and to plan relevant teaching strategies. It is important that you provide information to parents on the advice and services offered by your local authority and Early Years Development and Childcare Partnership (EYDCP).

In-service training and information

As SENCO, you will be expected to provide relevant training for your staff team. This does not, however, need to be delivered solely by you. The Early Years Development and Childcare Partnership plays an important part in supporting and training both SENCOs and early years staff, providing opportunities for individuals to develop skills and knowledge, helping them to provide support to staff in assessing and providing for children with special educational needs.

Funding should be available to help partnerships in training and providing area SENCOs who will offer support and guidance to setting SENCOs - so you will not be alone!

Additional support for the SENCO

Do not feel you should know everything immediately! It will be useful to draw up lists of relevant local and national contacts. Some local authorities compile their own SEN directories.

Contact experts for advice, or to provide staff training and make sure you go to all relevant training sessions.

The role of the SENCO is an important, demanding one, requiring commitment and a willingness to train and to be trained. You will probably have been chosen because of your interest and enthusiasm for the role, probably coupled with previous experiences and an understanding of children with special educational needs. Through this challenging role, you will be able to pass on your knowledge and understanding to others and provide a greatly enhanced service to children with special educational needs and their families.

Sue Fisher,
early years training consultant.

For more information see page 80 for Developing A Special Needs Policy, page 5 for Developing Inclusive Practice, page 15 for What Is Portage and Page 75 for Early Years & Early Years Action Plus.

Be Aware of Confidentiality!

The revised SEN Code of Practice (4.28) directs all SENCO's to Section 14 of the SEN Toolkit with regard to care and protection of 'sensitive' documents. Section 14 states that "confidentiality about certain issues must be considered". In line with the Data Protection Act 1998 be aware that documents such as IEPs and Child Information Records can contain personal and medical information.

All documents relating to a child should be:

- treated sensitively
- not left around
- stored securely
- not removed from the setting without the SENCO's permission
- shredded when finished with (after required archiving period)

All staff involved with such documents should be briefed/trained on Data Protection and how sensitive or confidential documents should be stored/signed in-out.

Check list for newly-appointed SENCOS

Familiarise yourself with:

☐ The Code of Practice

☐ Your setting's SEN policy

☐ Your setting's record-keeping systems

☐ Review your setting's system for assessment of individual children's progress and attainment

☐ Establish initial contact with your local Early Years Development and Childcare Partnership to identify training available

☐ Familiarise yourself with local facilities and support services

☐ Organise initial training for staff to ensure they become familiar with the SEN policy and the Code of Practice

☐ Assess resources available for children with special educational needs

Local contact numbers

EYDCP:

Educational psychologist:

Local children's centre:

Local Portage worker:

National contacts

National Association for Special Educational Needs (NASEN)
Tel: 01827 311500
www.nasen.org.uk

Council for Disabled Children
Tel: 020 7843 1900
www.ncb.org.uk/cdc

National Portage Association
Contact their administrator on 01935 471641
www.portage.org.uk

Kidsactive (formerly HAPA)
Tel: 020 7736 4443
www.kidsactive.org.uk

Developing inclusive practice

The Special Educational Needs Code of Practice states that the provision for children with special educational needs is a matter for everyone involved in each setting. As SENCO, under the overall direction of the head or manager of your setting, you will need to ensure that all staff members recognise and understand their responsibilities towards all the children in their care.

Why develop inclusive practice?
It is becoming increasingly accepted that inclusion is the right of every child, whether at pre-school or school. This helps to ensure that equal opportunities are provided for all. All children should be given the power of ordinary experiences and have the right to a broad and balanced curriculum.

Children with special needs will benefit from the atmosphere of a happy, stimulating early years setting. Children learn from doing things for each other and observing each other, and all children in the setting will benefit from working and playing with children with special needs.

Children can only be equal if differences are accepted. Therefore, ensuring your provision is inclusive to all children, rather than focusing on specific special needs, is an important starting point.

Supporting staff
The staff in your setting working with children with special needs will be responsible for their daily care. Some may lack confidence in this, but it is expected

that anyone looking after children should be able to manage a wide range of behaviours and needs. Staff members will also be expected to manage extra helpers working with the children, but at the same time can learn from such support workers who will often have specialist knowledge. Groups belonging to the Pre-school Learning Alliance, for example, may be able to access a support worker through their local branch to provide some one-to-one support. Other specialists, such as Portage workers and educational psychologists, may also be involved in the care of a child and staff will benefit from their experience and advice.

Action and adaptations
The Code of Practice states that decisions about which actions are appropriate

must be made on an individual basis, through careful assessment of the child's difficulties and their need for different approaches. It is vital to work closely with the parents of each child in building up a detailed picture of such needs. This will help you in being prepared to care fully for each child.

It is easy to fall into the trap of thinking you are including all children simply by accepting them into your setting, without making any changes. Therefore, as SENCO, a positive approach to inclusion is to identify what difficulties your setting may pose for children with special educational needs rather than looking at the difficulties their attendance may cause you.

It is often not particularly beneficial to provide special activities or equipment. What is more important is that staff use the information they have received from parents and other sources to adjust approaches to suit individual children.

The Code of Practice states that staff should enrich and extend the normal range of teaching strategies for pupils who may need extra help. For true integration, it is important for the children not just to be there, but to be part of it.

Examples could include:

- Story time: one-to-one support for a child who lacks concentration or whose behaviour may deteriorate in a group situation. Props and visual aids for children with hearing difficulties.

- Sensory exploration: This is strongly linked to working with children with special needs but is equally of benefit to all children, especially less confident children and those who find it difficult to express themselves verbally. A range of sensory equipment, both indoors and outdoors (visual, auditory and tactile), will provide valuable learning opportunities for all children.

- Adaptations to the physical environment: This is sometimes as simple as rearranging the furniture. For example, a less cluttered environment assists movement and extending the area of the home corner will provide play opportunities for children with mobility and vision difficulties. It is also important to keep the layout similar each time the child attends.

As SENCO, there are many ways in which you can support inclusive practice in your setting.

It will help you a great deal if all parents are asked to complete an initial assessment of their child's needs and progress to date. It is also useful to know about the impact of different disabilities. If possible, a home visit will give key staff the opportunity to see how the child is cared for and in particular to gaina better understanding of the care needs involved. This information will help you to help staff prepare for the child's entry to the setting. Remember also to focus on each child's strengths and achievements rather than what the child cannot do. This is a method of assessment familiar to all working in the early years and will encourage staff to have high expectations and set suitable targets.

Support and training

Make sure that staff have access to relevant support, information and training. Close links with your area early years development and childcare partnership are important as special educational needs and inclusion are priorities and they may be offering relevant training and support.

Local schools and other early years settings may also have experiences to share and could be interested in sharing training, ideas and resources.

Staff may worry that they do not have enough specialist knowledge to care effectively for some children. However, with training, advice, information and support this should not be a problem. Although it is your role to support staff, they should be encouraged to seek some information for themselves. You can support them in this by keeping details of useful contacts and addresses of organisations who will be able to provide useful written information. They may also be able to offer advice on how to make your setting more accessible to children with specific disabilities.

Bear in mind the differing needs of children when requesting resources. It is not always necessary to have special resources, but sturdy construction and small world equipment, for example, would be suitable for most children.

Overall, remember that inclusion must ensure all children are valued for who they are, andthe more flexible the strategies you

For further information on Art Therapy, Sensory Play and Play Therapy and Relaxation Techniques see page 17.

Organisations to contact

Centre for Studies on Inclusive Education.

National Association for Special Educational Needs (NASEN).

Disabled Living Foundation.

Full contact details for these organisations can be found on pages 87-88.

Publications

Good Practice in Caring for Young Children with Special Needs by Angela Dare and Margaret O'Donovan (Stanley Thornes) ISBN 0 7487 2871 6.

use,the more likely that children with a wide range of needs will make progress.

Sue Fisher,
early years training consultant.

Early identification and intervention

Some children will begin pre-school education already having been identified as having a special educational need (SEN) but a number of special needs will be identified for the first time whilst children are attending early years provision, with a significant chance that you or a member of your team (such as a key worker) will be the one who identifies it.

What is a special educational need?

It is likely you will first be alerted to the possibility of a SEN through observing that a child is not learning or behaving how you would expect for their age. All special needs will fall into one of the categories stated in the new Code of Practice. These are:

- Cognition and learning difficulties

- Behavioural, emotional and social difficulties

- Communication and interaction difficulties

- Sensory and physical difficulties

Why is early intervention so important?

The Code of Practice stresses the importance of early identification and assessment and places a requirement on early years settings to make sure that suitable provision is made for any child identified as having a SEN. You have a duty to recognise and identify any SEN in your setting and plan what action needs to be taken to help and support each child.

The same applies to those working in the private and voluntary sector.

How are special educational needs identified?

Many early years workers lack confidence in identifying special needs, yet have a wealth of experience in meeting children's individual needs. Some children will arrive at your setting already having been identified as having a specific

special need, but many more will not. Those already diagnosed are likely to have a label attached to their need and whilst this will help you identify what support they need, it is not imperative. What is important is early intervention to ensure the child reaches their full potential. As SENCO, you can support staff in understanding that it is their depth of knowledge of child development that assists more than anything else in the identification of a special need.

If a child is having difficulty, it is possible staff will be alerted to this early after admission. However, it is more likely that concerns will be raised when a child makes little or no progress, even when additional support has been given or when they consistently work or behave at a level well below that which is expected of a child of a similar age.

When concerns are raised about a child, it is important to gather together as much information as possible, from parents, records of assessment and, importantly, from first-hand observations of the child in a range of situations. A written format for recording initial concern is useful, in particular to help you and the child's key worker decide upon further action.

What next?

It is important to remember that the identification of a special educational

need aids appropriate provision and this is the key to early intervention. From your observation and assessment, it will become clear what each child needs and how they differ from others in the group and this information will help the key worker when planning and providing suitable activities.

The Code of Practice suggests that where practitioners consider a child has a special educational need, they should plan Early Years Action to meet those needs, aiming at overcoming the child's difficulties as far as possible. Many children will have their needs met in this way, as staff are able to use their experience of meeting the individual needs of all the children in their care.

Encourage staff to use the Curriculum Guidance for the Early Years Foundation Stage when planning appropriate provision. The ELGs help in clearly identifying components of tasks and these can be further broken down to produce smaller steps for children with special needs.

Throughout, it is important to talk to parents and involve them in your planning. This shared knowledge will lead to action and the earlier the action, the more effective it is likely to be in helping the child progress.

Sue Fisher,
early years training consultant.

Possible indicators of special educational needs

This list provides a starting point. It is important to stress to staff, however, that whilst a check-list can be a useful aid, their own experience and what they observe and understand from this is far more important than a label.

Cognition and learning difficulties

- Concern over fine/gross motor skills

- Language difficulties

- Difficulty following instructions

- Open to distractions

- Works slowly/poor output

- Makes more progress when individual attention is given or when tasks are broken down into small steps

Behavioural, emotional and social difficulties

- Tearfulness, anti-social, uncooperative

- Withdrawn, isolation from peers, preoccupied

- Aggressive, angry, disruptive

- Hyperactive

- Low self-esteem

Communication and interaction difficulties (including autistic spectrum disorders)

- Problems with communicating through speech

- Limited speech and vocabulary

- Frustration and anxieties

- Stammering, speech difficult to understand

- Difficulty in understanding meaning of spoken word

- Difficulty in following instructions

Sensory and physical difficulties

- Poor hand/eye coordination

- Inappropriate answers given to questions

- Immature speech sounds

- Poor sound discrimination

- Difficulty in some aspects of movement

Providing for all children: differentiation, consolidation and extension

Within any early years setting, there will be wide variations amongst the children in terms of development and maturity as well as family, religious and cultural background and special needs. All children joining your group or class will therefore have differing experiences, interests, skills and knowledge which will affect the way in which - and the pace at which - they learn.

You need to be aware of the importance of planning to meet a diversity of needs and to support staff in providing appropriately for all children in your care including those whose difficulties may be able to be addressed through a differentiated curriculum.

The revised Code of Practice states that a graduated approach should be developed to help children who have special educational needs. Differentiating the curriculum, thus providing for each child's needs, will be the first step in this model of action and intervention. All children within a group can be supported in their learning alongside each other, as long as staff are aware of as the differences in each child's stage of development and plan carefully, building on and extending children's knowledge, experiences, interests and skills.

Planning for all children

To endeavour to meet the needs of all children and aim for each child to reach their full potential, it is essential that teaching is planned and organised effectively to develop all children's knowledge, understanding and skills, while working towards the Early Years Foundation Stage themes.

Plans need to be flexible to allow children to be involved in different ways and at different levels, and whilst you should be aware of the learning intentions from activities, thorough consideration should be given to individual pace and style. These needs can then be used as a starting point for planning, reflecting the differing interests and developmental stages of children and setting challenging yet realistic expectations. The Curriculum Guidance for the Early Years Foundation Stage is a valuable document in supporting planning for varying developmental stages of children.

Putting plans into practice

When putting planned activities and experiences into practice, staff should maintain high expectations for each child, making sure that their existing knowledge and understanding is recognised, used and extended, and that challenges are meaningful as well as achievable, encouraging the children to think. Staff who have a thorough grasp of child development, and the needs of individual children in their care, will be able to implement the EYFS themes to pitch expectation correctly for the majority of children, matching teaching to each child's stage of learning and supporting their progression. For some children tasks may need to be broken down into more 'manageable chunks' so as not to overwhelm them.

Children sometimes also need to set their own challenges and practise and develop their own skills. In this way, they will gain an understanding of their own abilities and strengths.

Working with mixed age groups

Many settings work with a wide age range of children within the same group. For these the Curriculum Guidance will be of particular benefit in planning activities. In such settings it is particularly easy to fail older, more able children in an attempt to make activities accessible to all. By taking individual levels as a starting point for planning, staff can be confident that all children will learn from activities planned.

Sue Fisher,
early years training consultant.

The Early Years Foundation Stage

The Early Years Foundation Stage is based around four themes, each linked to important principles:

A Unique Child

- Every child is a competent learner who can be resilient, capable, confident and self-assured.

- Children develop at different rates, have different interests, come from varied cultural backgrounds and unique families.

Practitioners should ensure that provision reflects and supports all children. They should seek to know each individual child and their development, while celebrating interests and achievements along the way.

Positive Relationships

- Children learn to be strong and independent from a base of loving and secure relationships with parents and/or key people.

Practitioners should encourage respectful and caring interactions to promote emotional security which supports learning. This includes teaching conflict resolution through problem solving and discussing children's opinions.

Enabling Environments

- The environment plays a key role in supporting and extending children's development and learning.

Practitioners should observe, then organise spaces, materials and the flow of the day accordingly. Children need time, space and materials to play, investigate and explore.

Learning and Development

- Children develop and learn in different ways and at different rates - all areas of learning and development are equally important and inter-connected.

Practitioners should ensure there are challenging opportunities across all areas of learning. Experiences should provide stimulating opportunities to explore, be active, and think creatively.

The Department of Education Good Strategy guidelines suggest that the best outcomes for children's learning occur where most of the activity within a child's day is a mixture of:

- Unstructured

Play without adult support

- Child-initiated play

Adult support for an enabling environment and sensitive interaction

- Focused learning

Adult guided, playful experiential activities

- Highly structured

Adult directed activity with little or no play

Obviously too little adult support can hinder learning, but set sessions can be enriching. The same can be said for highly structured activity which can become overwhelming if it lasts too long... The secret is finding a blend. For example, short sessions of structured learning can be useful when teaching specific skills and can also benefit children with special educational needs.

Key ways that young children learn:

- Playing

- Being with other people

- Being Active

- Exploring new things and experiences

- Practising, repeating and applying skills

- Having fun

- Talking to themselves (self-speech)

- Communicating with someone who responds to their ideas

- Representing ideas and experiences

- Meeting physical and mental challenges

- Being shown how to do things

Learning through play is one of the key principles of Early Years education, especially when working with those with special educational needs.

Play develops positive dispositions for learning:

- Finding an interest

- Being willing to explore, experiment and try things out

- Knowing how and where to seek help

- Managing self, managing others

- Developing 'can-do' orientations to learning

- Being resilient – finding an alternative if something doesn't work

- Understanding the perspectives and emotions of other people

- Being inventive – creating problems, and finding solutions

- Being flexible – testing and refining solutions

- Being engaged and involved – concentrating and persevering even when a task is challenging

- Making choices and decisions

- Making plans and knowing how to carry them out

- Playing and working collaboratively with peers and adults

Families and practitioners should encourage children to play, pretend and be playful. Humour, creativity, exploration and interaction are invaluable when a child is learning.

Selena Ledgerton
Education & Childcare Consultant/Author

Publications

A full explanation of how to use the EYFS Themes can be found here:

Learning, Playing and Interacting: Good practice in the Early Years Foundation Stage Tool Kit

http://nationalstrategies.standards.dcsf.gov.uk/node/242798

Dukes, C. and Smith, M. (2009) *Recognising and Planning for Special Needs in the Early Years* (with CD-ROM), Sage, London

Working with parents of children with special needs

As SENCO, it is your responsibility to ensure that your intentions regarding working in partnership with parents are outlined in your setting's special educational needs policy and that this is reflected in practice throughout the setting.

The Code of Practice recognises the importance of the role of parents in their child's education. Parents know their child best. They have a wealth of knowledge and experience to share about their child's development and needs. Early years practitioners must encourage parents to share their knowledge and any concerns they may have, both about their child's needs and the provision being made for them.

Partnership in practice

For such a partnership to be achieved effectively, it is important that both parties recognise and value each others contributions. The Code of Practice recognises that parents have responsibilities for communicating with staff working with their child. Remind staff that they must always respect parents' views and opinions and be sensitive towards their feelings. Some staff members will probably need to work on their own communication skills and extend their understanding of working with parents, sometimes in difficult situations. As SENCO, you will need to monitor this and seek or provide suitable training if such a need should arise.

It is vitally important to remember the pressure that parents may be under due to their child's special needs. They may be experiencing feelings of guilt and rejection, resulting in a loss of confidence or self-esteem. Some, particularly where the child has an emotional or behavioural difficulty, may feel they have been held responsible for this and may appear angry or over-sensitive.

Encourage staff to develop empathy with these parents, helping them to feel at ease, and hopefully find it easier to share concerns about their child. Remind them that some parents may have great difficulty in coming to terms

with their child's special needs, and that approaches for dealing with these needs will differ. Some parents may place heavy emphasis on a child's disability, whilst others may play down their child's difficulties and emphasise the positive.

Whatever their own feelings, staff must respect all views and work positively and equally well with all parents. Even very young children are aware of how staff feel and respond to their parents. It is of utmost importance that staff value the input of parents and ensure they feel that their child is accepted and valued, too.

Building a picture of each child's needs

It is important to listen to parents' views at first to help you build up a picture of their child based on previous experiences. It is also important to establish what the child may think. This is usually difficult to find out directly with very young children, but it can be done indirectly through discussion with those who are closest to them. Before a child with special educational needs starts at your setting, arrange a home visit if possible to observe the child in their own environment. This also gives you an opportunity to discuss any issues with parents in a relaxed, familiar environment. Parents should also be given the chance to visit the setting on their own as well as with their child before the child starts to attend. This will help you when drawing up an individualised learning programme to take into account care and educational needs and provide targets and opportunities for them to develop in the six areas of learning.

After this, meeting with parents regularly, including informally, will help to ensure they are able to update you on their child's care needs and provide the latest information on others involved in their care such as Portage workers and speech therapists. Importantly, too, it will provide opportunities to share observations on their child's progress.

The timing of meetings and IEP reviews can be difficult for some parents. Many children attending private day nurseries have working parents and others may need to make childcare arrangements for other children whilst they attend a meeting. It is, therefore, important to take into account the individual needs of parents and be flexible about appointments.

Sharing achievement

Remember that it is just as important to share the child's achievements as it is to voice your concerns. It can raise the confidence and self-esteem of

both child and parents and could be as simple as drawing attention to the child's painting displayed on the wall, to a book or toy the child has shown particular interest in or celebrating a new stage of development the child has reached - for example, playing alongside other children or beginning to share resources.

Achievement for many children with special educational needs will need to be measured in much smaller steps than usual but this does not make their progress any less successful. Emphasise the child's strengths, sharing positive comments with both parents and child.

You will need to develop different methods of sharing achievement for parents who are not able to come in to your setting regularly. Many early years settings are familiar with home/nursery diaries and use these as an effective way of sharing information on the child's successes and experiences. This can be a valuable two-way link when it is not possible to have regular face-to-face contact with parents.

Parent partnership services and additional support

Make sure that parents are fully aware of the local parent partnership service and how they can get advice and support from this service. This service is offered by each LEA and aims to give practical, impartial advice to parents and carers of children with special educational needs as well as support and information which will help parents play an active role in making decisions concerning their child's education. The parent partnership service should offer a range of services, including access to an individual parent supporter for all parents who want one and putting families in touch with local support groups.

Individual parental supporters are trained volunteers who can also support parents in completing paperwork and accompanying them to meetings or on visits to schools.

Some local education authorities/early years development and childcare partnerships have produced their own comprehensive directories of local support groups and relevant organisations. As a SENCO, however, it is good practice to build your own directory of local and national contacts to support staff as well as parents.

Moving on

Throughout all stages of a child's early care and education, parental

involvement is essential and it is important that this continues when the child moves on to primary school. Records kept on a child with special educational needs, including individual education plans/learning programmes should be passed on to the school, with the parents' consent. You may need to explain the benefits to the child of passing these records on.

A strong partnership will develop if parents feel that their knowledge of their child and their opinions are listened to and valued and that they and their child are made to feel welcome by you and your staff team.

Sue Fisher,
early years training consultant.

Organisations to contact

Every Child Matters - Family Information Service

Contact a Family (CAF)

Advisory Centre for Education (ACE)

DIAL UK (Disablement Information and Advice Lines)

Home-Start UK

National Portage Association

Full contact details for these organisations can be found on pages 87-88.

Publications

Special Educational Needs a Guide for Parents & Carers has now been fully revised and is available from the Department for Schools and Families website: www.teachernet. gov.uk/docbank/index.cfm?id=3755.

It is also available by contacting: Department for Schools and Families Tel: 0870 000 2288 Email: info@dcsf.gsi.gov.uk

See Disorders section for further details.

Working with other professionals

Through developing relationships with a range of professionals and organisations, you will be able to build links between families of children with special educational needs in your setting and those people who are able to offer them support. For many parents, this will be a difficult time and by helping in this way you will not only be ensuring the best support possible for the child, but also for the whole family.

What role might other professionals play?

Where you have decided that children's needs can be met through Early Years Action, or when initial concern is raised about a child's progress, it is likely that your contact with outside agencies will be mainly an information gathering exercise.

For children whose needs will be met through Early Years Action Plus and for those with a statement of special educational needs, other professionals/organisations will be named on relevant documentation and should work in partnership with you to offer support for the child and join in setting targets for achievement.

For some children, particularly those with a statement of special educational needs, other professionals, such as Portage workers, may visit your setting to advise staff and work with individual children. A statement may also identify the need for a support worker who will be employed or sub-contracted by the local authority. Whilst their main role will be to support the child with special educational needs, everyone involved can reap rewards from this partnership. The most beneficial approach is for staff to work as a team in providing for all children, involving the support worker where possible, for example, in the planning of activities.

Establishing and maintaining contact

It is worth doing some homework to find out not only which organisations will be able to provide some support but also who the key people in each

department are and how they can be contacted. Getting in touch with them could be your first step towards building a successful working relationship. We all like to hear a familiar voice at the end of the phone so remember to keep a record of such contacts and keep this information updated as contacts change.

It is also useful to collect information on local resources, such as toy libraries. These can provide a wide range of equipment aimed at children with SEN.

Your Early Years Development and Childcare Partnership, LEA, health service or other local body may already have a directory of useful local contacts. A good starting point would be to contact those particularly relevant to the family you are working with.

If possible, display a selection of information leaflets from these groups. This will help to make sure that parents are not singled out and will provide helpful information when a parent suspects their child may have a special need or when this has been suggested to them.

Issues to consider

It will be beneficial to all parties if you:

■ Make sure you have a designated contact with lead responsibility for liaison with other professionals - this is likely to be the child's key worker

(alongside the SENCO) as they will have particular knowledge of the child's needs and be known to the parents.

■ Set up a regular means of two-way communication - consider informal contact by telephone/email as well as more formal meetings.

■ Invite them to review meetings - encourage involvement in both the meeting and participation in setting targets.

■ Make sure copies of IEPs are given/sent to all professionals involved.

■ Think about the timing of meetings - as with parents, remember those invited will have other commitments. It is good practice to find out what times are particularly good/difficult before arranging meetings. You will need to develop a flexible approach to involve all relevant parties.

The chart provided (see right) gives brief information on some of the professionals you are most likely to come into contact with. This list is not exhaustive and you will be able to extend this over time by adding your own. It should, however, provide a useful resource for recording and updating relevant contacts.

Sue Fisher,
early years training consultant.

Contact	Help available	Contact details
Educational psychologist	Helps to determine what child's educational difficulties may be and suggest relevant teaching approaches. Can also give advice on behaviour management (will always be involved if a child is to be statutorily assessed prior to a statement of SEN).	
Social worker	Can offer home support/assessment if needed.	
Speech and language therapist	Will assess child and offer advice to both parent and setting. May develop specific programmes for the child/suggest targets for inclusion on IEPs. May provide regular or one-off support dependent on need.	
Individual support worker	Provides help in developing and maintaining individualised programme of support for child (not necessarily 1:1 teaching). This support is often provided for children with a statement of SEN. Some EYDCPs/LEAs may also provide this for those without a statement – particularly for those with emotional/behavioural difficulties.	
Portage worker	Provides a home teaching scheme for pre-school children with SEN. Worker will assess child's level of development and decide which skills to work on next. May visit setting to observe how child behaves in a different environment.	
Physiotherapist	Provides support for children with physical difficulties/delay or poor motor control. Provides an individually planned programme of movements or exercises to be carried out at home/setting. Offers support and advice on specialist equipment.	
Clinical psychologist	Provides support, counselling and therapy for families. Can also offer advice on behaviour management, cognitive development and development assessment.	

What is portage?

Portage is a scheme for teaching pre-school children with special needs new and useful skills in their own home, through making their parents more effective teachers of their children. It originated in the USA in the 1960s, in Portage, Wisconsin, and was introduced into the UK in 1976.

There are now around 150 registered Portage services throughout the country that meet the criteria as laid down by the National Portage Association. Services work with children with a range of special needs, including Down's Syndrome, cerebral palsy, and autism, as well as children with visual or hearing problems and language delay or disorder.

Portage services vary considerably from region to region. They may be funded through education, health or social services, or be joint funded. A Portage team may include people from a variety of backgrounds, such as teaching, speech and language therapy, community nursing and health visiting.

Some services have volunteer home visitors; these are often past Portage parents. To become a Portage home visitor, you have to undertake a Portage Basic Workshop which lasts the equivalent of three days. It looks at the core principles of the Portage approach, as well as how to use the Portage materials to make assessments, to select teaching targets and long-term goals and to keep records.

How does Portage work?

Parents have a major role in choosing and carrying out the weekly tasks that encourage their child to develop skills in a variety of areas. During the first few weekly visits the home visitor and the parent will use the Portage checklist to identify what skills the child already has, those that are emerging and what the priorities are for the next few months. The checklist covers development up to the age of six in social, self-help, cognitive, motor and language skills, and a picture of the child's strengths and weaknesses is built up.

Together the parent and the home visitor decide on appropriate long-term goals, and activities to promote these goals are rehearsed each week for the parent to practise throughout the following week. These activities are written down on activity charts that carefully identify all the aspects that need to be considered, such as:

- a clear description of what the adult and child will do;

- what toys will be used;

- what help it might be necessary to give the child; and

- what rewards will be given.

The activity charts are used to record the progress during the week and over a period of time.

This might sound rather formal and clinical, but in practice it isn't. Parents

want to know what they can do for their child, but often feel they do not know where to start. It is often necessary to break down an individual skill into smaller parts that are more achievable, and this can be difficult to do at first. However, it is important so that even small steps towards the goal are recognised and celebrated. It is also important to recognise and build on the things that the child can do and enjoys, as so often the messages about the child have been negative and based on what he or she can't do.

The regular weekly visits mean that there is constant feedback between the parent and home visitor. The relationship that is developed through this contact means that some weeks the home visitor spends more time listening to the parents' feelings than talking about the activities, but this is a very important aspect of Portage support.

The parent and home visitor choose activities that are based on play, and which can be incorporated easily into the daily routines of the household. Other members of the family become involved, including brothers and sisters who often play an important part in the activities. Parents become more competent and confident about their teaching, more articulate about their child's skills and more aware of the different ways that children learn. As one parent says, 'The Portage method gave us the specific tools to help (our son) progress. No longer did I feel that we were working towards unobtainable goals, for I was helped merely to work towards the next, the closest milestone, and have confidence that having reached it, the following one would be attained as well. Looking back it seems as if there was a miracle, although I know there was a lot of hard work as well. Somehow the Portage activities never seemed a burden – we just included them into our daily routines and found that they served to enrich our family life.' (from *To A Different Drumbeat: A practical Guide to Parenting Children with Special Needs* by Clarke, Kofsky, Lauruol, Hawthorn Press 1989, ISBN 1 869890 09 4)

The positive reports of registered Portage services that have been inspected under the nursery education scheme have identified the strong partnership with parents and the effective assessment and recording processes as particular strengths.

What contact might Portage have with other settings?

When the time comes for a child to become involved in a group outside his home, for example his local playgroup or day nursery, you may well have contact with his Portage visitor. Effective liaison is one of the fundamental aspects of the Portage approach.

The home visitor could be involved in a number of ways. She might visit the group with the child in the initial stages or call in to see how things are going as time passes. She may discuss his current long-term goals with you, and how to approach some of them in your setting. This may be helpful to you when drawing up an individual education plan. She will ask for your observations of the child's progress in particular areas so that a full picture can be gathered, especially when it is time to review the long term goals.

Over the years the Portage model has been adopted in countries around the world and adapted into many different settings, other than the home. In response to the many pre-school children with special needs who are attending non-specialist provision, and in recognition of the implications of the Code of Practice for the Identification and Assessment of Special Educational Needs, the National Portage Association has produced a training package called *Quality Play*. The aim of the course is to raise awareness that all children, including those with a special need or disability, have rights to effective participation in a wide range of play experiences. It looks at ways to help practitioners working in group situations, such as playgroups and day nurseries, to develop strategies aimed at analysing and supporting the play of individual children of all abilities. The approach links closely to the stages in the Code of Practice.

There are continuous developments in the Portage delivery. For example, some services are looking at ways of extending aspects of the Portage approach as a child moves on into mainstream school, involving close liaison between the home visitor, parents and school staff. They have developed the Portage goals to include new skills needed for successful transition into school and they also provide training and ongoing support for teachers during the first two terms that the child is in school.

The National Portage Association works to encourage the principles that lie at the heart of Portage. As well as the Basic Workshop, which is open to people who may not be home visitors but who are interested in knowing how the Portage principles can be adapted into their setting, it is continually developing and monitoring further training modules. Examples include autism, play, early motor and communication skills, as well as aspects such as working with children with profound and multiple learning difficulties and the multicultural dimension of Portage.

Glen Cossins has worked for Gloucester Portage and was South West Regional Representative for the National Portage Association.

See page 11 for Working with Parents of Children with Special Needs and the Disorders section for further details.

Organisations to contact

National Portage Association

Full contact details for these organisations can be found on page 87-88.

Art therapy, sensory play & play therapy and relaxation techniques

Early childhood is a time of rapid growth and development and during these critical first years, young children enter a period where hands-on experience and play are vital.

With regards to working with children with special needs, it can be easy to dismiss art, play and relaxation as recreational rather than therapeutic and with that we lose a valuable resource.

These therapies can provide interest and stimulation for a child with mental or physical issues; they can soothe an angry child, offer a distracted child focus, be calming and relaxing and even provide a vehicle for communication.

So many children with speech or hearing problems love to paint how they're feeling or what they've been up to... and imagine how fantastic and fascinating an illuminated bubble tube is to a child who is visually impaired.

As is the case with all new strategies, it is a great idea to take a recognised course on these therapies with a qualified professional and do additional reading. I have included a reading list on page 25 and there are also numerous therapy courses available across the UK.

Try it for yourself and watch your child reap the benefits:

Art Therapy

The British Association of Art Therapists defines Art Therapy as "a form of psychotherapy that uses art media as its primary mode of communication".

The individual needs not be at all artistically talented, or even artistically inclined, and the art produced doesn't have to be aesthetically pleasing or accomplished. Instead, the basic premise is that irrespective of an individual's talent or inclinations, the very act of making art involves every human being in a creative process which is, by nature, healing, relaxing and life enhancing.

By offering children a chance to create, move and speak simultaneously, they have every opportunity to express themselves.

Art in itself is therapeutic and a form of 'self-talk'. It gives children a chance to show you everything from how they are feeling to what they would like to do next and all without words. They can share the things they love, the things they hate and as we discussed in the Emotional Management section, they can share feelings they never normally would... and it's a great way to relax!

For children with behavioural issues or special needs Art Therapy can also be a way of acting out any frustrations on paper (so put lots of newspaper down!)

and this in turn brings about a sense of calm as their erratic feelings have found a focus.

No matter what the child's need, your role is to encourage them, talk to them and ask appropriate and well timed questions ... we are looking to help children relax.

We are given an insight into their thoughts, beliefs and behaviours, while empowering the children we work with. Whatever they create gives them a sense of accomplishment "I made that myself" which raises self-esteem while nourishing confidence levels... and what a wonderful time to get to know your child.

Contact the British Association of Art Therapists www.baat.org if you require a registered therapist or are interested in training.

So what can I do?
Art therapy used for 'disclosure' or psychological and emotional issues should be conducted by a professional art therapist only as it requires years of training. But Art Therapy can also be used for children with special needs as a way to focus or relax.

Here's a list of art activities to try yourself. Depending on the child you work with you can then introduce your own based on need.

Remember that these are suggestions and the children should be allowed to take the lead and choose, with that in mind have a large selection of activities available to them per session.

Fingerpainting or Handprinting
Cut the images out afterwards and use them as leaves on a beautiful tree – add each child's name perhaps on a Christmas bauble, apple or conker.

Or print yellow, orange and brown hands to create a sunflower, if you add a stem it could be used as the base for a height chart in your setting - combining physical and creative with social and emotional development.

Painting
Free painting sounds too simple, but creating whatever they wish is one of the best ways for a child to relax (see the suggestions to follow if a subject is required).

Printing
You can use sponges, potatoes or string. Create pictures or elements for cutting and pasting. Or use printed shapes to make pictures (triangles and crescents to create a boat and its sails).

Try printing with round potatoes in multiple colours and then cut out to create one long caterpillar. Next, use painted string on a folded sheet of paper, pull out and create beautiful butterflies - caterpillar to butterfly, what an opportunity to discuss changes in nature.

Tactile Textiles
Dipping string in paint and squeezing out the excess can be messy but therapeutic. Pop the string into bright orange paint; squeeze the excess and leave to dry in swirls and spirals. Glue the strings onto paper plates and you have instant spaghetti for a display. Make some brown pom-poms or paper balls for meatballs – fantastic! There's no 'point' to this, no learning objective involved – that's the point. But if the children are responding well there's nothing to say you can't end the session with something.

Bubble Painting
Mix one squirt of paint with one squirt of washing-up liquid in a deep tray and add water... Hand the children a straw and let them blow!

Place sheets of paper over the bubbly water to create beautiful patterns on the paper, this can be used as water for a display, future activity or try cutting it into an oval and adding a white border... an instant bathtub that the children can stamp yellow ducks onto! Or why not paint green grass around the edge of their bubble sheet and they'll have their very own pond – Time to make some frog finger puppets!

Or you could simply cut out their name or initial.

Straw Painting
It's an old one, but a good one – have a sheet of paper ready with a blob of paint in the centre, hand the children a box of straws and let them blow. This is a brilliant stress relieving activity and it's fantastic exercise for the lungs!

You may also want to try this outside with a huge sheet of paper.

Edible Playdough/Playdough/Clay
WARNING: Always check your group's medical history for allergies before playing with anything edible and advise parents that this form of play is going to be introduced - if in doubt ask for written consent from parents and an update on any allergies in writing.

When working with children in their early years with special needs, clay and play dough are both fantastic mediums as they can be cathartic and therapeutic. The tactile nature of the dough alone can soothe and relax; the creative possibilities are infinite and the choice of colours endless. It's a perfect pocket resource.

An additional benefit is that it's such a creative medium. The children can be allowed to create whatever they like when in session and you can offer rolling pins, tools and cookie cutters as well as anything that makes an interesting mark or impression (if safe, age appropriate and the child's condition permits).

It's also re-useable. Have a camera handy and take photographs of each creation a child makes. Then you can encourage them to roll up their dough and start again (if they don't want to display their sculpture of course!) This way you have a record of everything they've made and you can both make a book together of the child's creations. They can look back on everything they've created which is great for self-esteem and positive reflection. You can also discuss each piece with them and point out all of the things they did well.

The Munchies!
If your children are used to working with standard playdough then that is great, but if you are having problems with children trying to eat the dough then there are numerous edible recipes available – you just have ensure that the work area is as sterile as a baking session!

WARNING: If you are unsure if your child has nut allergies do not use the recipe below. Always check for ANY allergies before using anything edible in session and be aware of choking hazards.

Peanut Butter Play Dough (Use on day of making only)
2 heaped tablespoons of peanut butter
1 large mug of ready oats
(powdered 'brek' type)
1 tablespoon of honey
½ tablespoon of pre-boiled water
(for consistency)

You can even use a cookie dough recipe (egg-free) and advise the children that if they each cut out a cookie as they play, you'll bake it for them later...

Food colouring can be used to create edible dough in different colours, but be aware that the E numbers in such colourings can affect some children's behaviour. Check with parents and medical histories before use. Do not use if children are prone to hyperactivity.

Just a thought: Take photographs of all of the children in your setting and laminate them. If you cannot add each child's name to the elements they have created on the display then add a small laminated sheet at the base of the image marked 'ARTISTS:' and tack a photo of each child who has participated to the Artist's Board. This idea works wonderfully for any display or behaviour boards.

What about discussion?

Before we get to discussion, it's important to remember that we are using Art as a form of relaxation and focus and are not 'probing for information'. Art therapy used for 'disclosure' is conducted by professional art therapists and requires years of training. If you are concerned in any way by the images a child creates, speak confidentially to your line manager and follow your settings child protection procedures.

Questions:

"What are you making?"

"How lovely, tell me about your picture?"

Point to a tree or other object and say "Is that me?" (you know it's not, but a joke is a great way to break the ice and encourage communication)

"Who's that?"

"Is this you?"

"What colour are you using next?"

"Why did you choose this colour?"

"Can I paint with you/next to you?"

"What a beautiful painting/sculpture/collage."

Don't forget to display some of the artwork at the children's eye level and be sure everyone's work is represented.

Play and Sensory Play Therapy

Play Therapy uses a variety of play and creative arts techniques to alleviate psychological, physical or emotional conditions in children which symptomatically cause behavioural problems, distress or stress and prevent children from realising their potential.

Play therapy can be practised in various ways, as it can be directive – where the child is guided in play, non-directive where they are able to choose or a mixture of the two.

One of the best examples of non-directive work comes from Virginia Axline. In her

book *Dibs in Search of Self* she describes working with a disturbed young boy. He cannot use the word 'I' as it feels unsafe and refers to himself as Dibs in the third person - "Dibs will play now" or "Dibs feels sad". Over a period of time Virginia Axline allows the child to play and explore the world in a safe environment. She allows the child to set his own pace, never directing his play and following his lead. The child makes a remarkable recovery.

Much of current play therapy practice is based upon Virginia Axline's work. So much so that Axline's Princifamilies are still used as guidelines for non-directive play therapy today:

Axline's Principles

The therapist:

■ Must develop a warm and friendly relationship with the child.

■ Accepts the child as she or he is.

■ Establishes a feeling of permission in the relationship so that the child feels free to express his or her feelings completely.

■ Is alert to recognise the feelings the child is expressing and reflects these feelings back in such a manner that the child gains insight into his/her behaviour.

■ Maintains a deep respect for the child's ability to solve his/her problems and gives the child the opportunity to do so. The responsibility to make choices and to institute change is the child's.

■ Does not attempt to direct the child's actions or conversations in any manner. The child leads the way, the therapist follows.

■ Does not hurry the therapy along. It is a gradual process and must be recognised as such by the therapist.

■ Only establishes those limitations necessary to anchor the therapy to the world of reality and to make the child aware of his/her responsibility in the relationship.

Whatever the approach, Play Therapists use a wide range of play and creative arts techniques, mostly responding to the child's wishes.

Play Therapy Activities include:
■ Art

■ Creative Visualisation

■ Storytelling

■ Sand Tray

■ Music

■ Dance & Movement

■ Drama Therapy

■ Puppets

■ Masks

■ Clay

Play Therapy is particularly effective with children who cannot, or do not want to talk about their problems or issues.

The Play Therapist is required to be empathetic and form a short-term therapeutic relationship with the child. The work often involves dealing with the child's social environment (parents, teachers, peers and family) and when working with children with disabilities or special needs, clinical supervision is essential.

Filial (or non-directive) play can also help children with special needs in their early years. This form of therapy draws additional help from the child's family and allows both parents and carers to be trained in basic play therapy skills (if they so wish). This means that both home and setting are working in unison, using the same techniques – and in turn providing further stability for the child.

The issue with this form of filial therapy is whether parents should be administering therapy at home or if it's better for the child that the home environment remain a family environment rather than an academic or medical one. In other words, no evaluations in the living room please!

Rather than give direct training such as this, Play Therapy United Kingdom prefer to provide coaching and mentoring for parents and carers on how

to develop their nurturing skills and play non-directively with their children.

Training to become a PTUK Certified Play Therapist requires successful completion of accredited Certificate and Diploma Courses (APAC).

What can I do?
Get training or ask a professional play therapist to join your team.

Training opportunities, contact information, play therapy models, strategies and suggestions are available from Play Therapy United Kingdom. www.playtherapy.org.uk

But in the meantime if you would like to make a start, you should review Axline's Principles and with an open mind offer the child in your care a selection of the play therapy activities previously mentioned.

Considering we spend an awful lot of our time directing children, it's difficult at first to do nothing and let the child free-play but like Axline, allow the child to set their own pace, resist directing their play and follow their lead.

You may also want to look into developing a 'Play Space' or 'Quiet Place' within your setting.

Set aside a small area of your setting or separate small room. This area can be filled with everything from cymbals and drums to a sand tray with a rake.

A 'Play Space' is useful if a child is frustrated and wants to act out. They can bang, crash and play loudly with whatever toys they choose. A 'Quiet Place' is somewhere a child can reflect, think and meditate. They can push the sand around in the tray, float leaves on the water or simply cuddle a bear.

(See Sensory Play & Art Therapy sections for more ideas.)

Sensory play
Sensory play is play that involves the use of one or more of the five senses: touch, sight, smell, taste and hearing.

Our senses help us to fully experience the world around us and for young children they provide opportunity for amazing discovery. Watching a colourful bubble float away, hearing a baby cry, smelling a flower, tasting a mouth-watering strawberry or touching a silk ribbon are all opportunities for sensory learning.

To truly discover the world every child should experience new things with all of their senses. In the case of a child with special needs, this is even more important as they may have had limited opportunities to do so in the past or been unable to fully experience the world because of need, disability or mental/developmental issues.

All children need to see, hear, feel, touch, smell, and sometimes even taste whatever they are learning about in order to understand it fully. Our responsibility is to provide these sensory opportunities as often as we can so children can experience and learn from all angles...

What will they learn?
When playing with the various sensory toys, activities and materials a child may:

■ Improve their fine and gross motor skills via moulding, pouring, sorting, folding, carrying and filling.

■ Develop their creative skills as they play freely and use their artistic talents to cook, sculpt or paint with the sensory media they are using.

■ Increase their self confidence by mastering what they are trying to achieve.

■ Improve their social skills by working as part of a team, learning to share materials, taking part in discussions and learning new words (in turn increasing their vocabulary).

■ Develop their cognitive skills by problem solving, making observations, performing experiments and manipulating the materials given.

■ Learn colours; develop counting skills, and experience sequencing, sorting, construction.

Sensory play is not just messy play (which unfortunately many believe). To take that approach is unfair to the child as some children don't enjoy messy play and can be put off by it. The prospect can even cause them stress which would defeat the object.

Sensory play is about using the senses, exploring different materials, phenomenon, objects and substances and experiencing them via sight, smell, sound, taste and touch. The children's eyes, nose, ears, tongue and fingers shouldn't know what's hit them.

Sure, sensory play takes a little more thought and planning – but it's worth it and its great fun!

The Eyes

- Pull faces in a mirror.

- Visit the 'bendy' mirrors at the funfair or local playplace.

- Play with light reflections on a wall using a mirror.

- Use multiple mirrors to reflect one object and 'see how many you can make'.

- Draw whilst looking in a mirror (try drawing half a simple smiley face and making it whole – a great early symmetry class too.)

- Play peek-a-boo games under a blanket to experience light and dark or under a brightly coloured parachute in the summer.

- Watch sound by pouring dried beans onto a speaker, or by using a tuning fork or a dancing flower to witness movement from music.

- Play with brightly coloured blocks, shapes, beanbags, cars, Stickle Bricks™ or puzzles. Ask questions referring to shape and colour to make the eyes and brain work a little harder – "Can you find the red heart-shaped bean bag?"

- Play with a colour-change bubble tube, torches or fibre optic lamps/wands.

- Make a rainbow mobile using CDs, crystals and prisms – in the sunlight it will cast rainbows on the wall and sparkle brilliantly!

- Play with brightly coloured toys.

- Offer coloured transparent sheets, sunglasses, 3D glasses, binoculars and magnifying glasses and let the children take a look at the world in a whole new light!

- Fill secure containers and bottles with different interesting and colourful items, such as water & glitter, beads, coloured water, bubble mixture, pom-poms, coloured pasta, rice and lentils. A child can shake the glitter suspended in the water like a snow globe or even stand one coloured bottle in front of another to learn about mixing colours – red and blue to make purple.

- The Memory Game: lay out 5 to 10 items, allow the children to look at them for 60 seconds and then take one away. The children have to guess which one has been taken. An alternative to this is that you cover up the items and ask them to recall all 10.

- 10 Clear Bottles: Pour water into 10 bottles and stand in good light. Allow the children to experiment by dripping in different food colourings with a dropper to see what effects and colours they make – then offer them vegetable oil and washing up liquid to drop in too and see the liquids move by themselves!

- Visual overload: Visit the library, beach, shops, park, zoo, museum, observatory anywhere a child's eyes can be stimulated by the view (and their other senses will spring to life too!) Talk to your child about what they can see and discuss colours, names of objects and how different views make you feel. Exposing a child to new experiences keeps them curious about the outside world.

The Nose

- "Smell the air and tell me what you can smell."

- Cook with the children and point out the fabulous odours.

- Ask what food smells the children like and which they don't.

- Guess the smell: Ask a child to close their eyes and offer them wonderful things to smell. Try using foods, flowers, scented soap or a drop of aromatherapy oil on a cotton ball – vanilla, lemon, mint, and lavender.

- Visit a farm, a park, a garden centre or bonfire, anywhere that smells can be identified.

- Introduce scented candles or aromatherapy sticks to stimulate a child's smell. (Ensure they are stored safely away from the children when lit.)

- Ask the children what their favourite smells are, or even to bring you their favourite smell on a cotton ball in a jar. (It's best to get parents involved in this so you don't get any surprises.)

The Ears

- Use listening and noise-making activities together.

- Watch sound by pouring dried beans onto a speaker or use a tuning fork or dancing flower to witness movement from music.

- Play with musical toys or those that vibrate.

- Play music during sessions and encourage teaching staff/colleagues to use music to start and end the day (at least) – low volume classical music is wonderful during reading time.

- Make a homemade orchestra. Use containers and lentils for shakers, spoons, pans and boxes for percussion and drums and elastic bands stretched over a tissue box as a guitar. The children will have just as much fun playing the instruments as they do making them! If you want to go the whole hog, make a milk bottle xylophone using different levels of water. The children can strike the bottles or blow across the top of them to make sound.

- Offer music of varying tempo and genre each week.

- To encourage motor skills, get the children moving and dancing to music or play music with lyrics or rhymes that the children will know and they can act out what's happening as a form of expression.

- Offer roll out musical mats for the children to dance/step on.

- Provide a musical instrument box.

- Take the children on a 'sound hunt'. Give them a list of sounds to listen for and as you walk around they can tick them off. Alternatively you can all listen for sounds and make a chart of the sounds your group heard. Try this in different places and see how the sounds change. Is what you hear at the seaside the same as what you hear in the town?

- Make a lotto game using pictures of animals for example and as you play the sounds the children mark the animals off their lotto board. The winner is the one who fills their board first. You can also use transport, people and places for other sound lotto boards.

- Introduce the children to different volumes and sounds. How about some relaxation music or whale or jungle sounds for instance?

- Play a game where the children try and identify sounds – prepare a tape of animal sounds, seaside noises and everyday knocks and grates.

- SING! Counting songs, animal songs, alphabet songs, songs about transport, colour, shape, holidays and events – the list is endless. You can sing alone, as a group, with music or without.

- Put different items into secure containers and see if the children can identify what's inside by the sound it makes when shaken. Try sugar, buttons, lentils, cotton buds/balls, shells, sand, paperclips and stones.

The Taste buds:

- Children understand flavours best when they cook. Plan some kitchen time and introduce different tastes from different places around the world.

- Bake some delicious biscuits with icing and sprinkles – all edible.

- Allow the children to experience and identify a range of tastes for example, hot and cold, sweet, sour, spicy, salty and fruity.

- Use raisins or small foods when practising counting, for every question a child gets right they can eat one!

- There are many simple cooking activities: try mixing ingredients to make muesli, icing fairy cakes, decorating cookies with chocolate chips or sweets, drawing with icing or melted chocolate on rice paper, making popcorn, filling jacket potatoes or topping mini pizzas. And how about printing a recipe for smoothies using images of fruit and have the children help you make a jug for the group?

- Get creative and make breakfast cereal collages using peanut butter as glue (check for allergies) or cereal hoop necklaces on a sweet lace.

- Put chocolate coins in a tub of jelly and let the children hunt for them.

- Create sculptures using edible play dough. (See the section on Art Therapy for a handy recipe!)

- Ask the children to identify food from taste alone, use different juices and foods.

- "Taste this, can you guess what it is?"

- "Now taste this, can you guess the two fruits that are in it?"

- Give the children opportunity to distinguish between tastes – Offer similar fruit juices and see if they can tune their taste buds and identify the flavours.

The Hands & Fingers:

- Develop sensory perception through touch.

- Play popping bubbles!

- Finger and hand painting (see Art Therapy for additional ideas).

- Utilise the sensation of warm and cold.

- Touch guessing game: is it hard, soft, wet, dry? What is in the box? Try using a dishcloth, sponge, silk, scourers, fur or rose petals.

- Share and read touchy feely books.

- Create sculptures using edible play dough. (See Art Therapy for a handy recipe!)

- Put chocolate coins in a tub of jelly and let the children hunt for them.

- Try dry textures too – cotton wool, beads, gravel, shells, pebbles, sand, potato flakes, oats, peas, beans, sugar, salt, buttons, materials, satin, fleece, wool and many more. How about hiding some of the larger items in sand or flour and let the children identify them by touch. The children will have great fun sieving them out as well and that in itself is another form of sensory play.

- Use PVA glue in a squirt bottle to make cobwebs or window pictures on cling film (add a little paint for colour) – peel them off and stick them up. Great for Halloween when black and sprinkled with silver & green glitter.

- Explore textures - this is not just about messy play.

- Water tray with coloured water and items sunk to the bottom. Ask the children to identify the items by touch alone.

- Offer soft pillows, furry bears, fleece blankets and hot water bottles at story time.

- Weave with satin ribbons.

- Make a touchy feely book with the children.

- Visit a soft play area with padding, balls, soft puzzles, slides and mats, lots to touch and feel. Let the children get 'squashed' between the padded rollers and 'popped' by the foam balls.

- Go on a touch and feel walkabout - experience rough bark, smooth shells, crispy leaves, prickly holly, wet dew and tickly grass. Take a collection tin for leaves, pebbles and shells etc and how about doing some bark rubbings so you can see texture as well as feel it.

- Use scoops, sieves, pots, spades, moulds and buckets with the sand tray. After dry sand play, add water for a different experience and don't forget to make a proper moat so the children can feel the cold water too.

- Messier sensory substances for play include jelly, water, shaving foam, condensed milk, beans, cornflour gloop, wet sand, compost, mud, wet pasta, papier-mâché, baby lotion and mashed potato. Items can be hidden within these substances or they can be poured, sieved, bottled or potted.

The most important thing to remember when working with children with special needs is that sensory play is about finding a way.

No matter what needs, issues, disabilities or problems a child has, they have the right to experience the world like every other child. Your responsibility is to make sure they can.

Here's some examples:

If a child in your care has a visual impairment for example and you're doing sensory play for the eyes on colour, then discover/research what the child can see and build from there - this is all about the positives. If their eyes can pick up bright light, offer them a lit bubble tube that changes colour for instance.

Or you can use alternative senses: if a child can't see the waves lapping on the beach, he can still hear them and feel them – time for a day trip? Or if a child has a hearing impairment and cannot enjoy the music you are playing for the group, lay a speaker flat on the floor and pour on some dried beans so the child can see the vibrations - the higher the bounce the deeper the beat. They can also lay their hands on the speaker to feel for themselves.

The idea is that you find a way regardless of need – this is inclusion in a nutshell.

(See Play & Art Therapy sections for more ideas...)

Relaxation Techniques

The word 'relaxation' fills some practitioners with dread as it conjures up an image of 20 children sprawled on the floor fidgeting when they're supposed to be relaxing. Fortunately these boredom busting techniques are tried and tested and some incorporate movement, dance, music and visualisation into the session – there's even a list of music.

*Always consult a GP and parents - ensure that all children are physically fit and able to take part before beginning any physical exercise.

Techniques for children

Deep Breathing: Deep breathing is beneficial for everybody. Start by introducing a child to slow breathing, taking a deep breath and releasing and then breathing slowly while counting to ten. This is great for a child's blood pressure, heart rate and wellbeing, but also a great way to calm a child or create a focus. (Also see Progressive Muscle Relaxation, Meditation and Yoga)

Progressive muscles relaxation: This involves focusing on different muscles in the body and then relaxing them in a progressive way. For example you can focus on the arms, stretch them, hold them and then release them at the same time that you release your breath.

Or you can try a group relaxation session.

Here's an example script: lie down, close your eyes, breathe deeply and relax. Imagine you are lying on a cloud and with each breath you sink deeper and deeper into the soft fluffy cloud. Deeper and deeper... (Pause and allow the children to breathe). Deeper and Deeper... (Repeat four times) Now... you are completely relaxed, imagine a warm orange glow above your head. With each breath it warms and sooths, sending wonderful relaxing energy into your body, washing away all of your stress. Slowly but surely the glow moves slowly across your head it warms and relaxes your forehead, then your brow... it relaxes your eyes ...and warms your face.

This can continue this so the orange glow moves down the body and relaxes all of the muscles. On completion advise the children to open their eyes, sit up slowly, stretch and smile. They should remain sitting for a while before they stand.

(Relaxation Script taken from *Meeting Special Needs: A Guide to Support Children with ADHD* by Selena Ledgerton Cooper, Step Forward Publishing)

Visualisation: Visualisation is another very useful way to relax, a child can imagine beautiful places, with peace, happiness and people they love.

Exercise: Low impact exercise helps boost circulation and general health, but it's also a relaxation tool. Walking and holding/releasing poses are two activities which can release tension from muscles without being stressful.

Stretching: Stretching is fantastic for releasing tension.

Meditation: A wonderful way for children to relax:

■ Ask the children to sit with their legs crossed and hands on their knees.

■ Ask them to imagine a beach in their mind with their eyes closed.

■ Prompt them every 20 seconds: Imagine every detail...

Can you see the sea...
Can you hear the sounds...
The birds...
Sit down on the sand and let the water tickle your toes...
Take some deep breaths as the water laps at your feet....

■ Play some relaxing music and allow the children to drift...

Positive Reflection: Sitting in a calming environment and discussing all of the things a child CAN do well. This is a real positive exercise for any child but highly beneficial for children with Aspergers, Autism or ADHD for example.

Massage: Obviously for child protection reasons massaging a child in your care is not advisable. But massage is a great form of therapy and relaxation and should your child require regular massage then you should discuss training with your line manager or request a professional take your child for set sessions (following a review with the child's parents and practitioners).

Dance/Expression: The children are encouraged to dance or express themselves through movement to a slow but uplifting piece of classical music e.g. Morning from 'Peer Gynt' by Grieg

Musical appreciation: The children lie still and relax during a piece of interesting music (breathing slowly) and then sit up and discuss what they heard and how they feel. It's a great way to focus and relax as the children really have to clear their minds and really listen.

Classical music with animal sounds, weather or intriguing noises are great for this:

■ *Flight of the Bumblebee* by Nikolai Rimsky-Korsakov

■ *Beethoven's Sixth Symphony*

■ *Cloudburst* from 'The Grand Canyon' Suite by Grofe

■ *Swan Lake* by Tchaikovsky

■ *Morning* from 'Peer Gynt' by Grieg

...and if you want to make the children happy you can include a track from a popular children's animation to close the session. This will also provide opportunity to stand, stretch and smile, ready for the rest of the day.

Yoga: Yoga works the brain as well as the muscles. It aids concentration and is lots of fun!

It can:

■ develop strong, flexible and healthy bodies

■ set a lifelong foundation for well-being

■ foster creative expression and imagination

■ increase focus, concentration and attention span

■ cultivate self-esteem, setting patterns of success and achievement

■ cope with stress more effectively

■ relax and sleep better

■ teach anatomy and physiology

Here are some examples of child friendly yoga:

Big Balloons
"Put the palms of your hands together at the centre of your chest. Close your eyes, and begin by taking three big balloon breaths. When you breathe in deeply, raise your arms up above your head in the shape of a big balloon. Then breathe out and bring your arms back down so that your palms are together at the centre of your chest." Repeat 5 times.

Puppets
"Lie down on your back. Imagine your arm is connected to your leg by a string and when you lift up your arm (straight) your leg comes up too. Breathe in as you lift, breathe out as your arm and leg go down. When your arm is up, stretch straight up toward the sky." Repeat 5 times.

If the children are older, this exercise can be adapted so they use alternating arms and legs.

There are numerous books and websites available providing appropriate yoga exercises for children. Give it a go; you'll love it, and so will they!

*Consult a GP and ensure that all children are able to take part before beginning any yoga sessions. In addition, contact a qualified Yoga Instructor for advice and instruction before practicing and demonstrating yoga.

Following a relaxation session it's always a good idea to 'bring the children back' ready for work (unless they're heading home). You can use any focus exercise you like, but one exercise that always works well is Brain Gym.

Brain Gym

Brain Gym, developed by Paul E. and Gail E. Dennison, is a "series of simple and enjoyable movements that we use with our students in Educational Kinesiology to enhance their experience of whole-brain learning".

The movements involved are many but here are two that are very simple and suitable for children in their early years.

These exercises can help to improve writing, spelling, listening, reading and comprehension, as well as coordination, breathing and stamina, concentration and spatial awareness.

*Always consult a GP and parents - ensure that all children are physically fit and able to take part before beginning any physical exercise.

Cross Crawl

These are contra-lateral exercises which requires alternate arm and leg movements.

- Reach behind the body to touch the opposite foot.

- Crawl across the floor in slow motion. Raise one hand and the opposite knee at the same time, alternating hands and knees. (Great for balance too!)

- Touch one hand to the opposite knee, raising the leg, or touch the foot, raising the leg. Implement 10 reps once a day.

Lazy 8s

This allows for crossing of the visual midline. Midline movements work to increase upper-body coordination (for gross motor and fine motor skills), improve bilateral movement skills and help to further activate the brain.

The child should line up with a point at eye level, and then draw a lazy 8 (an 8 lying on its side), the larger the better. Then the child follows the 8, three times with one hand, three times with the other, and then both together.

Rather than a finger, 8s can be drawn with:

- Dry-wipe markers on white boards

- Using scarves swirled around

- With water and brush on sugar paper (this dries and can be used again)

Brain Gym can also be accompanied by music. After a relaxation session this should be upbeat and uplifting so as to encourage the children to wake and focus. www.braingym.org.uk/

When you offer a child any of the above activities, you are working in line with Every Child Matters:

- be healthy

- stay safe

- enjoy and achieve

- make a positive contribution

- achieve economic well-being.

And building on the EYFS Early Learning Goals:

By discussing muscles and parts of the body during relaxation sessions and including movement and exercise you are adding to a child's Knowledge and Understanding of the World and encouraging their Physical Development. By using Art or Play Therapy as a form of focus or relaxation, asking questions and encouraging a child to engage, communicate and play, you are nurturing their Personal, Social and Emotional Development as well as their Creativity.

Selena Ledgerton
Education & Childcare Consultant/Author

Organisations to contact

Art Therapy

The British Association of Art Therapists

Focusing

Brain gym

Play/Sensory Play Therapy

Play Therapy United Kingdom

Relaxation

Relax Schools & Relax Kids

Full contact details for these organisations can be found on pages 87-88.

Publications

Art Therapy

Introduction to Art Therapy
Judith A Rubin
Routledge 2009
ISBN: 978-0-415-96093-9

Play/Sensory Play Therapy

The Handbook of Play Therapy and Therapeutic Play
Linnet McMahon
Routledge 2009
ISBN: 978-0-415-43941-1

Fun with Messy Play
Ideas and Activities for Children With Special Needs
Tracey Beckerleg
Jessica Kingsley Publishers 2008
ISBN: 978-1-84310-641-8

Dibs in Search of Self
Virginia M Axline
Balentyne Books 1986
ISBN: 978-0345339256

Special Education in the Early Years
Ruth A Wilson
Routledge 2003
ISBN:0-415-30347-8

Relaxation

When My Worries Get Too Big
Kari Dunn Buron
Autism Asperger Publishing ompany 2006
ISBN: 978-1931282925

Focusing

The Thinking Child
Nicola Call
Continuum International Publishing Group, 2003
ISBN: 9781855391215

Emotional literacy

A child's ability to learn relies on their ability to manage personal and social tasks. If they are unable to understand and express their emotions or be self-aware with regards to their needs, their work will suffer. To build relationships children also need to be aware of others, what they are feeling and how to communicate. Otherwise they will have few friendships and little in the way of social support.

For children with special needs, self-esteem is a big issue!

Frustration builds up when they cannot complete a task as it seems too difficult, complex or overwhelming and this makes them feel like an underachiever or a failure. Relationships with others may also be difficult as they can feel isolated, 'different' or misunderstood, because of their disorder.

Children can benefit greatly when they understand their emotions and feelings. It sounds strange but it is a skill to be able to share your emotions and convey them to others. Many children find this very difficult as they are self-aware and don't want to sound 'silly' or 'mushy' in front of their friends. This can be overcome if Emotional Literacy is used as a class-wide strategy. If it is introduced and everybody does it, it will soon become commonplace.

Discussing feelings can begin at circle time. The children can take a 'smiley face' card or 'sad face' card from the centre of the circle and talk about a time they felt happy or sad. As time goes on, new faces can be introduced to the pack – Anger, Upset, Shock, Joy and many more.

Create a collection board on the wall of your setting and start collecting 'feeling' words. Note down any that the children come up with too and put them up. You can take the children over and refer to this board if they are looking for a word to express how they feel.

An important time to use Emotional Literacy is when two children argue or disagree.

Sit the children down and ask them to "take turns and use your words please." It's surprising how well the technique works, even in nursery. If they need a prompt offer them, "I feel...." and then "because..."

In this situation a toy or bear can be used as a turn taking tool and the child holding it can explain what happened and how they feel. They then pass the bear to the other child so they can have a turn.

This is also a great strategy if a child is upset. Being encouraged to use their words and explain what is wrong alleviates stress.

"Don't keep your problems on your shoulders, they may crush you. Let them float from your lips and fly away..."

Emotional Literacy is also about teaching how to resolve issues, so be sure to help the children be 'good listeners', and when the turn taking has ended ask, "What can we do to make them feel better" or "How can we fix this problem?"

When working with children with special needs, emotional literacy can play a significant part in achieving goals and building self esteem. Children begin to understand that they can share how they feel and express what causes them to be frustrated and unhappy (and most importantly that someone will listen). They become more expressive and can say "I need to take this step by step" or "I need help", and this helps avoid frustration and in turn emotional or physical outbursts.

Developing a child's emotional literacy can help encourage expression and reduce frustration - See Disorders Section for further details.

Case Study

Whilst working in a voluntary aided Primary School, I worked one-on-one with a child with ADHD for three months before his emotional literacy began to develop. Previously, he would rarely speak to others and would physically erupt if he became frustrated. After discussing basic emotions, we talked about frustration and he described it as a tense feeling 'like holding my breath'. I advised that if it felt as if he was holding his breath, he should be sure to breathe deeply and calmly when he felt like that, and raise his hand to let me know. He said he did not want to raise his hand in front of the class, so we agreed that as a calming technique he would breathe deeply and count to ten inside his head (and move his head from side to side as he counted). This way I knew the child was frustrated and needed attention (via the physical signal) and he had a way to calm down at the same time. It took a long time to get to that point, but it was a real breakthrough for him and me.

Selena Ledgerton

As a professional it is also important to remember that you can influence a child's emotions without even realising it. Words can be weapons and it's easy to make a child feel isolated, especially if they are vulnerable. Rather than using "you" haven't done this or shouldn't be doing that, I try saying "what can we do to get going on this task, shall we break it down" or "I was hoping we ALL would have started by now."

The response will always be more positive if you are positive and the class reaction may come as a surprise. You may find that the other children look around to help those who haven't begun; the child in question may begin working step-by-step or realise they should have started and look to you for help if they are 'stuck'. Children respond well to not being isolated by the word 'you'.

Remember to share how happy you are with the group when they work well, engage quickly or behave. Expressing your own emotions verbally sets a good example for the children to emulate, and nurtures their emotional literacy.

Important: emotional literacy is a skill that may take time to develop in a child with special needs. The concept cannot be forced, it must come naturally. So the idea of sharing feelings should be promoted and repeated individually as well as with the class. A child with special needs may have been bottling their emotions for many years and may find it hard to express their feelings freely. They may even have specific emotional issues depending on their circumstances (you may need to discuss this with their psychologist if that is the case).

Emotional Literacy is about understanding your emotions and acting on them. If a child can comprehend how they feel (inside) and can recognise that feeling as frustration, they can let you know before it becomes too much. Once they can recognise an emotion, this opens the door for you to introduce anger management strategies, relaxation techniques and much more. (See the Therapies section for more information on this.)

As an additional technique (which works well with coaching), you may want to encourage the child to verbally reward themselves. Advise them of their good behaviour and ask them how they feel. Encourage them to give themselves a pat on the back and think "I did a good job!" This raises self-esteem and gives the child a sense of pride. In the future you can also extend this to cover longer or connected tasks. "I did a good job on that picture, now I'll do my writing and show Miss."

By learning and applying these techniques in the classroom, a child's emotional development can be nurtured. Children can benefit from greater emotional awareness, more emotional control and relationship building skills. This in turn leads to higher self-esteem and emotional intelligence.

Selena Ledgerton
Education & Childcare Consultant/Author

Including disabled children: practical ideas for play

Inclusion defined

So what are the main areas that need considering when looking at the development of inclusive early years or play services? The starting point has to include reaching out to parents of disabled children, spending time building up relationships, and listening to what they have to say. It is only through working in partnership with parents, carers and disabled children that good quality inclusive practices can be established.

To be truly inclusive a play environment must address three fundamental components - access, participation and activities - and we will examine each of these in turn. Many supposedly inclusive play environments provide access but fall short on participation. It is no good allowing disabled children to attend if you do not have the appropriate resources to enable them to participate. Making play environments inclusive means that we must examine the types of experiences available to the majority of children and ensure that those experiences are also available to disabled children.

Access

Clearly physical access for children with mobility difficulties is an issue although the majority of disabled children do not use wheelchairs. In most cases minor alterations can be made which are relatively cheap and can improve physical access. Organisations such as the Centre for Accessible Environments can help in this process. Most pre-school settings can already accommodate pushchairs and so need no adaptations in terms of level entrances. In some cases more permanent physical alterations will be required - such as the provision of suitable toilet facilities.

Access is not just about physical access to buildings but also about ensuring that the needs of visually impaired children are taken into account, and that signs and information is provided in large print and Braille. Colour codes and picture symbols can also be used for children with learning difficulties.

Over and above this, access is about having the will and the commitment to include disabled children. This is far more important than ticking off points on a check-list and declaring your project accessible. Dealing with needs as they arise and making every effort to include and welcome all children is central to this process.

Participation

Some children will undoubtedly need extra support or help with communication in order to participate - children with challenging behaviour and children with physical disabilities such as cerebral palsy in particular. Children who will not participate or whose behaviour seems inappropriate or obsessive may also need to be encouraged and supported to try out new activities. But you don't need to be an 'expert'. Rather you need practical information from parents such as "How does the child communicate?", "What are her likes and dislikes?", "Does he need any special equipment for feeding?", and so on.

In order for children with speech and language difficulties to participate they need to be able to communicate. There are many methods of communication apart from the spoken language (British Sign Language and Makaton, for example) and it is important for staff and for non-disabled children to be aware, and have some knowledge of these methods. This can be encouraged by, for example, involving children in games and songs which involve signing - all children seem to love this!

It is also important to provide some training for staff. The charity Kidsactive (formerly HAPA) provides training nationwide on inclusive play and can adapt training packages to suit the needs of early years workers in pre-school settings. There are also a number of organisations offering disability equality training. However, most nursery staff will find that they already have many of the skills needed to work with disabled children, the essential attributes being sensitivity, adaptability and imagination.

Activities and resources

Play environments must support play experiences that are matched to children's developmental levels and are also individually appropriate. Thus activities and resources must offer a variety of active learning experiences which are geared to the needs of disabled children as well as children from ethnic minorities.

Special toys and play equipment for disabled children are rarely needed, though are useful. Try using standard equipment with some small adaptations, or toys with sensory stimulation which are naturally inclusive. The organisation Action for Leisure can advise on all aspects of toys and resources that are appropriate to varying ages as well as disabilities. The other alternative to buying is to borrow - in the UK there are around 1,000 toy and leisure libraries for disabled children run by Playmatters, the National Association of Toy and Leisure Libraries.

For further information on Art Therapy, Sensory Play and Play Therapy and Relaxation Techniques see page 17.

Organisations to contact

Kidsactive (formerly HAPA)

Action for Leisure

Parents for Inclusion

RNIB

National Deaf Children's Society

MENCAP

Centre for Accessible Environments

Full contact details for these organisations can be found on pages 87-88.

Managing children's behaviour

Children need to learn, often through trial and error, how to behave in an acceptable way in a group setting. However, good behaviour cannot be taught in isolation from the rest of the activities but pervades everything going on in the group. It is important not to see behaviour as a separate issue, but within the wider context of the group, as an integral part of the learning taking place and the overall organisation of the sessions.

Children's behaviour is also influenced by wider social, emotional and cultural factors. How children behave will depend on how the group is organised, the planning of the daily routine, the quality of the activities available, the choices on offer and the quality of the interaction between the adults and children and between the children themselves. Children's behaviour is closely related to relationships. Other factors such as partnership with parents and carers will also have an impact on the children's behaviour in the group.

As the way children behave is such an important factor in their learning, each early years setting should have a written behaviour policy, which is often referred to as a discipline policy. However, managing children's behaviour is not simply about 'discipline', or 'getting them ready for school'. Discipline in the pre-school situation is about having order within the group. It is not about orders to be mindlessly followed, but about helping the children understand right from wrong and helping them learn to behave in appropriate, socially acceptable ways for the rest of their lives.

What is a policy?
A policy is a working document which clearly explains the group's philosophy, procedures and approaches to managing the children's behaviour on a daily basis. The main reason for having a written policy is to share this information with all those involved in the group to promote consistency. If adults are clear, consistent and fair the children will benefit.

It is important that those involved in carrying it through in practice have ownership of the policy. In other words, the policy should be something to which staff, parents and even children should have an input, not something written by or imposed from above, or some sort of standard list produced by an organisation or copied from another setting.

A staff meeting is a useful time to brainstorm ideas. A draft could be sent to parents for comments. Each policy will be individual to each group and the content should be developed and discussed by all staff, in response to the group's needs and circumstances. The length of the policy will vary from group to group. The main point is that it should be clear, practical and easy to understand. The whole idea is for unwanted behaviour to happen as little as possible.

Who is a policy for?
The policy is for the benefit of anyone involved in the running of the group. This includes the staff, parents, volunteers, students, any management committee and, ultimately, the children in the group. A policy provides clear guidance for the adults in the group on procedures for encouraging wanted behaviour and dealing with unwanted behaviour. Whilst children are often accused of being very good at 'playing adults off' one against the other, they are actually testing out the consistency of boundaries that

are being set and can feel confused by inconsistent responses. To give a simple example, if only two children are allowed at the sand tray and one day someone allows three children to play, they become confused, especially if another adult then appears and tells them off! It is important for children to have a minimum number of clear rules which are consistently applied. These could be attached to or included in the policy. Some simple rules can be displayed in pictorial form using matchstick people. Typically, these might include points of routine organisation such as 'four in the sand tray'.

If parents are given a chance to read the policy, they will be clear before their children start attending the group about the procedures which will be followed and any support available in the case of a child with a particular difficulty. The parent may then choose to adopt similar procedures in the home to support the work of the group.

A policy is also a valuable tool for allowing outside agencies, such as Social Services or Ofsted, to see that the group is professionally managed and has given careful thought to this element of learning.

Last, but most important, the children themselves will benefit from the policy. Through its implementation, they will learn the difference between acceptable and unacceptable behaviour and they will learn to take responsibility for the consequences of their actions. They will be helped to develop self-control, respect for the needs of others and respect for property.

What should the policy contain?

Although there is no model policy, here is a guide as to what clear statements to include:

- an overview of your group's approach, aims, philosophy

- procedures for encouraging acceptable behaviour

- procedures for dealing with unwanted behaviour

- procedures which are unacceptable for managing behaviour

- any agreed rules

- name of person to contact in case of concerns

- date produced or reviewed

Remember to make sure that new staff are aware of the policy. Staff could be asked to sign to say they have read and agree to implement the policy. It is also important to reflect on how it is working in practice, to review and if necessary update the policy from time to time. Once the policy is in place it needs to be translated into practical situations in the day-to-day organisation of the group.

Caroline Jones, nursery owner and part-time lecturer at the University of Warwick

See page 15 for information on Portage, page 11 for Working with Parents of Children with Special Needs and the Disorders section for further details.

Organisations to contact

Numerous websites and forums are available for behaviour support ideas. E.g. www.foundation-stage.info

Sample policy - Happyland Pre-school Group

Overview

Happyland sets high expectations of behaviour through encouraging and praising good behaviour. At Happylands we encourage children to respect themselves, each other, adults and property. We apply simple rules fairly and consistently. We aim to provide a happy, caring environment with challenging activities. Under no circumstances do we use any form of corporal punishment. In the case of a particular incident or persistent unacceptable behaviour we always discuss ways forward with parents. Our agreed rules are clearly explained to the children and are on the parents' noticeboard. They are based on the following principle:

- unwanted behaviour is behaviour likely to hurt, injure or upset another child, himself or an adult. Unwanted behaviour shows a lack of respect for others, disrupts their play and learning or damages their property. Below are our procedures for managing the children's behaviour.

Positive procedures for encouraging good behaviour

- prevention – anticipation and removal of potential problems (stop the fight before it happens!)
- interaction – plenty of adult attention (so that there's no need to misbehave to attract attention!)
- praise or reward – all adults should offer explicit praise for good behaviour, for example turn taking, co-operation, sharing, listening . . . drawing attention to the good rather than the bad
- provision – provide physically challenging and emotionally satisfying activities for children to 'let off steam'
- clear expectations applied in a positive way – 'No pushing in the line' becomes 'Stand nicely'
- leading by positive examples from adults.

In certain circumstances, such as racist language, physical abuse or dangerous behaviour an instant adult response is required.

Procedures for dealing with unwanted behaviour

- redirection – distract to another activity or join in with activity
- a firm 'No' and a clear explanation of why the behaviour is unacceptable
- speak calmly, clearly and firmly to gain control
- give a warning of the consequence if the behaviour does not stop
- use the consequence, for example, removal from the situation, or removal of the toy
- a fresh start afterwards

Unacceptable procedures in managing behaviour

These should never be used and, if seen, would and should be reported immediately to the person in charge. Such conduct could result in staff dismissal.
- shouting, criticism and comparison. Shouting conveys a loss of control.
- labelling the child, rather than the behaviour, as 'naughty' or undesirable
- use of any form of corporal punishment, including smacking, pinching, poking or rough handling
- use of any other humiliating and frightening punishment, including shouting, offensive language, name calling or isolation.

Named person - If you are concerned about any child's behaviour or our responses, or have any other comment on this policy please contact:

Date: ....

Establishing better behaviour

If a child is misbehaving, the first thing adults need to consider is whether the child is misbehaving deliberately or might there be another reason for his actions. Sometimes adults need to step back and consider the cause of the unwanted behaviour, particularly if a child's behaviour changes from being normally co-operative to difficult. Other reasons for so-called 'naughtiness' may include:

Expectations or language not matched to stage of development

Interaction with children must take account of their stage of development. Young children can only cope with a limited amount of instructions at any one time and may not be being deliberately disobedient but genuinely not understand what is expected. For example, a child who has limited comprehension or auditory memory will not understand a complex series of instructions such as 'When you've finished, hang up your apron, wash your hands, go to the toilet and then go into the other room' and may end up looking blank when he or she is then told off for not going into the other room. The same child would have responded appropriately to one or two instructions at a time.

Sometimes they are being asked to do a task which is not matched to their level of understanding. In other words the task is too hard or too easy and they become frustrated, perhaps resulting in a tantrum or a squabble. They may not have heard the instruction the first time and need it repeating. Sometimes, they do not have the language to understand the instruction in the first place. It is easy for an adult to become frustrated or cross when a child appears not to be doing as he or she was told. For example, the instruction 'Find a space' often results in children wandering around all over the place. Is the adult sure the child knows what a space is? Is the child walking around looking for it? Often a child can be labelled naughty for something which is merely developmental, for example, wetting pants, not sitting still for long, lack of attention, when maybe he or she is just not ready or able to do what is being expected.

Sheer physical exuberance

If there is not enough outlet for a child's energy he or she may run around, start crawling under the tables, or climb on the furniture. It is important to ensure that if the children cannot go outside, perhaps due to the weather, some alternative form of energetic activity is provided indoors.

Insecurity

Children become confused if adults are inconsistent. They feel insecure if expectations are not made clear or something which is acceptable one day is not accepted the next day. They become confused if the routine changes for any reason or staff changes are taking place. Offering children an open choice may also result in confusion. 'Who wants to go first in the line?' will lead to chaos, whereas with 'It's John's turn to be first

today and Joanne's tomorrow' everyone knows what they have to do.

Illness

Often a change in behaviour can be a sign of developing illness. The child does not feel right but does not know how to express the feelings. He or she becomes miserable and uncooperative, even cheeky. The next day the child develops an ear infection or breaks out in spots!

Anxiety

Factors outside the group's control may have triggered the unwanted behaviour. Those working with young children are all too familiar with changes in behaviour when something is amiss at home which has upset the child in some way. It may be a way of releasing anxieties – the death of a grandparent, arrival of a new baby, a parent leaving the family home, fear of starting school. Children should be happy and develop relationships with adults and with each other which minimise negative behaviour. If they are encouraged to express anxieties and ask questions the need for anti-social behaviour as a response to anxiety is reduced. Any sudden change in behaviour should always be shared with the parents and monitored carefully by a named adult.

Anger

A child who is tearful or clingy or having a tantrum is not necessarily being naughty. Tantrums, for example, are very common among toddlers. The child has not yet acquired a sufficient grasp of language to express himself in words. The need to assert independence spills over into a tantrum. A tantrum is a very powerful feeling of anger and frustration and often the child needs comfort combined with restraint. A tantrum is a child's (and some adults'!) way of expressing very strong emotions. Inability to cope with people, things or situations is often the cause. Those working closely with children will recognise a tantrum from a child who is using a loud noise to attract attention and trying to control the adult or getting his or her own way. Responses may vary and will depend on the circumstances. Try to find out what is making the child angry. Often a child's anger can be redirected through playing with dough, role play, hammering pegs, banging a drum, or going out in the garden. Withdrawal to a quiet place or a little cuddle will help him or her regain control. The important thing is for the adult to remain calm and once the tantrum has subsided, to make a fresh start.

Testing the boundaries

Prevention is better than cure and many things can be avoided if the circumstances which trigger the unwanted behaviour are avoided in the first place. Of course, children will still explore and experiment to find out where the boundaries lie between acceptable and unacceptable behaviour. Where the situation or the adult is unfamiliar they will experiment with different kinds of behaviour until it becomes clear where the line is drawn. Often children look straight at the adult before actually doing the 'crime'! The absence of consistent boundaries leaves children insecure, dashing about waiting for someone to control them. Often they are labelled hyperactive, when really they are seeking boundaries to control their behaviour. Once the children have discovered what is allowed and what isn't allowed and the same rules apply all the

time, they will be satisfied and direct their energies elsewhere.

Positive strategies

Unacceptable behaviour in the pre-school is usually defined as action which interrupts the child's own learning or the learning of others, harms another person, themselves or property. Within a context of positive preventative strategies unwanted behaviour can be dealt with through light control methods, although in some cases stronger measures may be called for. Light control is appropriate in a situation which requires minimum intervention.

One example of light control is where attention is focused on the rest of the group, sometimes known as positively ignoring. This will often succeed in reminding the 'targets' who a few moments later can also be praised for behaving as they should. This will work in everyday situations such as the following:

Example - A child pushing in a line

A negative response would be to say "Jack, for goodness sake, stop pushing!"

A positive response would be to say "Robert, Sarah and Emma are standing very still in the line. Well done!" Then, if Jack stops pushing. "Well done, Jack! You're standing beautifully as well, good boy!"

Example - All the children are listening to a story, a few start to fidget

When a child is fidgeting instead of listening attentively, again praise for those who are listening is far more effective than constantly drawing attention to those who are not listening. The idea is to explicitly draw attention to the majority of children who are conforming to the acceptable norm.

Example - At drinks time

"Look how quietly these two tables are sitting" is much more likely to produce wanted behaviour from the third table, than "Table three, you're the worst table in the room."

In addition, it is important that the adult makes the desired behaviour clear. Telling children clearly what you want them to do is far more effective than telling them to stop doing something. "John, stand still" is much clearer than "John, stop running". Children need to be told in language which they understand and are not confused by.

Distraction is also likely to produce the desired behaviour. If a child is picking

The adult's words and manner must be firm and leave the child in no doubt as to what will follow. Be fair, be clear, be consistent.

1 Gain attention

2 Say what the unwanted behaviour is

3 Say why the behaviour is unacceptable

4 State the action warranted by the behaviour

5 Give the instruction which implements the sanction

her nose, for example, instead of saying "Don't pick your nose!" say "Wiggle your fingers!" As I'm sure you know, if children are told not to pick their noses, the automatic response appears to be to start picking again a moment later!

Rewards

Where there is a specific behaviour which a child is struggling to achieve, rewards may be effective in the short term. However, it is important not to overrely on rewards. The adult has to remain in control and be the decision maker. For example, when a child has really made an effort and listened extremely well to the story (for him) he can be offered a reward. However, it is important that the adult is not bribed by the child, or does not put the child in control of the reward. For example, if the adult says, 'If you sit still you can have a star' then the child is in control. However, the adult could say, 'I may decide to give someone a star if someone sits beautifully.'

Alternatively, the adult may say nothing and observe the child closely. On spotting 'good behaviour' the adult will then reward the child and explain why. "I saw you sharing that puzzle, well done, you can have a sticker". Below are some types of rewards which are used:

- Social rewards - pleasant interactions such as a smile, praise, clapping, hugs.

- Activity rewards - having a go on the computer, choosing a song, choosing a story, playing a particular game.

- Token rewards - stars, stickers

- Material rewards - edible or usable items - such as a biscuit.

Discipline should be about positive re-enforcement of acceptable behaviour and positive role models. If a child is shouting and an adult responds by shouting at the child then the child will not understand that shouting is unacceptable.

Stronger action

Major incidents are fairly unusual. At pre-school level a child may hurt another child, for example, by biting, pinching, hitting, pulling hair or throwing sand or throwing a toy. In these situations stronger action is needed.

- Deal immediately with it - do not leave it until later.

- Avoid getting into battle with the child or a confrontational situation.

- Use the child's name but beware of giving the child a label.

- Forgive and forget.

The child who has been attacked must be comforted and the child who is at fault helped to see the reason for adult intervention, without feeling attacked or undermined himself. In all circumstances children need to know the consequences of their misbehaviour. Use of consequences is an objective approach - if you spill the paint, you will wipe it up, if you drop your coat on the floor, you will pick it up. The adult's tone of voice can have a major impact on children's behaviour. There is a major difference between shouting and speaking firmly. "Oh darling, please, you mustn't bite", in a kind and gentle tone of voice will not give the message that biting is unacceptable.

Example 1

1 Jack

2 Throwing things

3 Can hurt people and

4 You will sit on the chair for a minute

5 And think about what you should have been doing.

In case of persistent misbehaviour adults can employ a warning procedure. Firstly, give a reminder of the rule: 'We do not throw sand'. Then a brief warning of the consequence: 'You will not play in the sand'. Then, if the behaviour persists, follow example 2.

Example 2

1 Jessica

2 Throwing sand

3 Can hurt people

4 You will not play in the sand

5 Come and have a think about it.

If a major incident does occur which requires strong words or action, which may even make the child cry, it is a good idea to record it in a book. If a child tells a parent "Mrs Jones got cross with me today", the parent may phone up wanting to know what's happened. It is professional to take the parent quietly to one side and explain the incident.

After an incident, if the child has the language, the adult should ask the child to tell him or her what caused the incident and ask "What would be a better thing to do?" If the child then is spotted doing the right thing, this can be acknowledged with a comment such as "Jack, I'm pleased to see you're taking turns. That's good - your mum will be pleased. Do you think you can keep it up? I think so."

Other strategies include:

- Checking the physical setting - are they squabbling because there is not enough? Have they learned to share? Where is the adult?

- Changing the context - is it time to change the activity? Has the child been on the activity too long? Is it time to tidy away and get something different out?

- Providing help - for example, with a jigsaw puzzle thrown on the floor. Pick it up with the child and do it together.

- Changing the organisation - if the cars on the table are causing a problem, moving them onto the floor can diffuse the situation.

Whilst to say 'Come and sit on this chair and have a little think' may just help calm a situation, the use of a 'naughty' chair as a sanction is usually ineffective and not acceptable.

Physical handling

The physical handling of children is a sensitive area. On rare occasions staff in groups can be accused of physical assault. The existence of a behaviour policy should clearly stipulate no use of corporal punishment or any other action which will frighten or humiliate a child. This would also include not only smacking but pinching, squeezing, hair pulling, isolation, putting a child in a cupboard or anything likely to cause emotional upset to the child. The adult must show that only 'reasonable

physical restraint' was used to calm the situation and in particular to prevent the child from harming him or herself. For example, if a child was running towards a road or climbing over a fence and likely to fall, the adult would have no choice but to physically handle the child. If staff have attended relevant training courses and a comprehensive policy is in place, there are unlikely to be any problems.

A small minority of children do have emotional or behavioural difficulties which cause higher levels of concern. The parent should be consulted and perhaps seek advice from the health visitor, who in turn may recommend the support of an educational psychologist. Strategies available include the drawing up of detailed individual programmes, personal counselling, therapy or focused support.

In summary, then, children's behaviour is very complex but there are certain things that are known to encourage good behaviour. These are:

- clear rules
- praise
- showing correct behaviour
- consistency
- consequences
- preventing
- reinforcing good behaviour

Acknowledgments
Some of the material for this section has been drawn from Solity J and Bull S (1987) *Classroom Management Principles to Practice* published by Croom Helm and Finch G *Handling Children's Behaviour* NCH Action For Children.

Caroline Jones,
nursery owner and part-time lecturer
at the University of Warwick

See page 15 for information on Portage, page 11 for Working with Parents of Children with Special Needs and the Disorders section for further details.

Organisations to contact

Numerous websites and forums are available for behaviour support ideas. E.g. www.foundation-stage.info

Identifying and supporting more able children

In Africa there is a saying: 'When you plant a tree, never plant only one. Plant three – one for shade, one for fruit and one for beauty.' This may also be sound educational advice. In a world where there would appear to be increasing pressure to excel, it may be that practitioners are planting only one tree – we see children in terms of their ability to be 'fruitful' or 'achieve' school targets.

With the advent of Early Intervention and the publication of documents such as the Curriculum Guidance for the Early Years Foundation Stage, we are becoming more and more aware of children who might be called 'intelligent', 'bright' or 'more able'. Identifying some of these children will be easy – 'I can read that book myself' – but I would suggest that being more able is more than just being able to read, write and count ahead of what might be expected.

What does it mean to be more able?

Each of you will have your own ideas about what it means to be more able. The language we use, our personal experiences, the media and culture we experience, will all have shaped our concept of what a more able child can do.

Our ideas influence what we believe children are capable of. For example, do you believe intelligence is fixed? If you do, then this is likely to mean that you will not believe a child is capable of growing and improving. If a child believes this, then they will give up when they fail, believing that they can't get any better – 'I'm not clever enough'. On the other hand, if you think that problems are to be solved then you will believe that intelligence is not fixed but able to grow – 'I can improve if I practise' – and children, too, will begin to think this way.

Another topic worth exploring as a staff is in which areas of the curriculum are children most likely to be identified as more able. Miss X, the key practitioner in the pre-school setting, may think it's about abilities in a range of curricular areas.

Mr Y in Reception class or primary one may think it's about maths and language. Mrs Z, as the head, may think it includes aesthetic subjects – music, drama, art, PE. These different perceptions will influence how they present the curriculum. Coming to some kind of shared understanding about what intelligence is and how it is demonstrated will help to establish that everyone is working towards the same goal. It will also help to make sure that you recognise, celebrate and value a range of abilities. The first step for any setting may be to decide what they understand by the word 'intelligence' and what abilities constitute a child being identified as more able.

Pointers

There are a number of pointers that might lead us to think a child is more able. They may, for example:

- show advanced development in the area of thinking skills – they are imaginative and creative, they can read, write and use numbers in a well-developed way;

- display a definite learning style – they are motivated and inquisitive, they can work independently, they have good concentration;

- have highly developed speech and language skills – they can use metaphors, carry out instructions, have a good vocabulary;

- develop early motor skills - they know left and right, they can complete difficult puzzles/jigsaws, they can take apart and rebuild objects;

- demonstrate well-constructed social skills – they have an understanding of the rules, an ability to form close friendships or an interest in social topics.

As with any checklists there will be children who don't fall into these categories. Stereotypes about more able or intelligent children can blind

practitioners to children who do not fit traditional ideas. So, checklists can be helpful, but only if used with caution!

We know that high quality early education is vital to children's development. If we are going to enhance learning, we need to build on prior learning. If children are displaying certain abilities then we need to find out what those are and then challenge them. Going through every ELG in order to get to the end may not be helpful and will certainly not be challenging to young enquiring minds. Underachievement can be the result where lack of challenge prevails; this has to be avoided.

Types of intelligence

Having agreed that we should be catering for children who demonstrate abilities, I would suggest that the question practitioners need to be asking

is not 'How smart are you?' But 'How are you smart?' Answering this question will naturally move us away from traditional views that intelligence is narrowly based on maths and language abilities and towards a wider approach where a variety of abilities are included. Howard Gardner (1983) suggests that there are eight intelligences:

- Word smart
- Maths smart
- Music smart
- People smart
- Self smart
- Body smart
- Picture smart
- Nature smart

We all have at least three areas of strength from this list. Profiling the children with whom we work across the seven intelligences will produce jagged results. This will allow us to see where we need to continue to challenge, but it will also allow us to see where we need to develop certain skills. If children enter settings with a range of abilities which are not challenged then the result may be underachievement.

Offering a curriculum for young able learners may prove to be challenging. We have to acknowledge that they need the same kind of demanding activities that older children require but at the same time be age appropriate. 'More of the same' is not a helpful strategy. However, too difficult a task may also result in boredom. Our understanding of the child and his or her abilities is crucial if just the right amount of challenge is to be offered. More able children will often crave an intellectual peer with whom they can share their thoughts and ideas. When this happens children will often seek out adults in the setting. The adult has to ensure that they don't simply give the child answers whilst at the same time meeting the needs of all the other children in their care. As I said, a challenging task!

There seems to be a general concern about the effects of 'hot housing' children or indeed of labelling them: 'too much too soon'; 'we'll turn them off'; 'they'll not have any friends'. Whilst too much too soon can indeed be damaging, it is perhaps not so much that the children have been identified that creates the problem but more the misuse of the information we receive that can lead to difficulties. It is therefore vital that we

plan a curriculum that acknowledges and values abilities, wherever these may lie.

Play is a wonderful way of offering learning experiences. Young children play naturally and derive enjoyment from the experience. We must therefore consider what the child will gain from the play experiences we are providing. Young able children, and indeed all children, should be involved in planning their curriculum. This encourages responsibility for their own learning and increases motivation. Young able children can be capable of working on their own. However, because they can 'get on with things' they are often left to do so with very little interaction with more knowledgeable others. It is important to ensure that any interaction between the adult and the child is of a high quality. Planning this interaction is vital.

Interaction with adults

Given that time is always of the essence we should consider the role we will embrace during the interaction. Will we be giving instructions? Will we be assessing? Will we be posing questions? Care should also be given to the way in which we respond. Are we creating an atmosphere of trust and mutual respect?

Of course, these suggestions are good for all children. However, some activities will seek to offer children broader and deeper learning experiences through open-ended tasks, abstract concepts, complex

ideas or the teaching of thinking skills. As has been noted by Callahan (1996), 'It is extremely difficult to build a strong differentiated curriculum on a weak basic curriculum'. It is therefore important to establish that you are offering a strong basic curriculum before developing strategies for young able children.

If we concentrate on only one area of development and we see children in terms of their ability to be fruitful or achieve, we may be planting only one tree. On the other hand, by valuing and celebrating a range of abilities, we will help to make sure that we are planting three trees – one for shade, one for fruit and one for beauty.

Margaret Sutherland,
lecturer, Faculty of Education,
Glasgow University.

Organisations to contact

NAGC For Gifted Children and their Families

Full contact details for these organisations can be found on pages 87-88.

Attachment disorder

Attachment is the deep connection established between a child and parent in the first years of life. It profoundly influences every component of a child's life from how they react to affection, to how they build relationships themselves.

Attachment is not something that parents offer a child, but rather something that parents and children create together over a period of time - a long-term reciprocal loving relationship.

Babies will instinctively reach out for the safety and security of their parent and a young child looks to a parent for care, guidance, support and boundaries.

But what if this is missing? And worse still what if a child is abused or neglected?

Reactive Attachment Disorder or RAD (also known as Attachment Disorder) is a condition caused by events that occur early in a child's life. These events mean that the child is unable to create attachments due to a disturbed attachment cycle and negativity results.

In real terms, as a child grows they learn quickly that their caregiver is not reliable or unable to tend to their needs. In turn they believe that they can trust no one and must protect and care for themselves. With the loss of trust comes negativity, and anger is internalised. As the child gets older parents will have problems setting boundaries and disciplining the child as that initial trust is not there. The child has no reason to think that the parent cares, is looking to protect them or working in their interest when they set boundaries - they protect themselves by rejecting rules set.

The table on the following page outlines the likely causes, symptons and long-term issues associated with attachment disorder.

Treatment
The most important treatment for a child with attachment disorder is for them to have an emotionally available attachment figure. Children can take

part in attachment therapy which can involve working on behaviour, emotion, connection and affection with their attachment figure. Psychological therapy is also required so that the child has the opportunity to discuss the present, and more importantly the past.

Some children may also be offered medication for depression or behavioural problems.

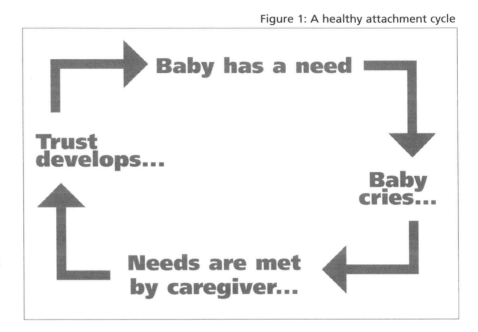

Figure 1: A healthy attachment cycle

Baby has a need

Trust develops...

Baby cries...

Needs are met by caregiver...

Figure 1: An unhealthy attachment cycle

Baby has a need

Trust does not develops. Upset, negativity and anger...

Baby cries...

Needs are not met by caregiver...

Possible causes	Possible symptoms	Long-term problems
Parental: Parent or carer changes Parental separation Abuse and/or neglect Ineffective and insensitive care Family frequently moves Depression Severe and/or chronic psychological disturbances: biological and/or emotional Young or inexperienced parent Substance abuse Traumatic experience Maternal or Postnatal Depression History of separation Loss or death Maltreatment Prolonged absence through a parent in prison, hospital or desertion **Child:** Traumatic experience Difficult temperament; lack of "fit" with parents or caregivers Premature birth Medical conditions; unrelieved pain (e.g. inner ear), suffers from colic Hospitalizations: separation and loss Failure to thrive syndrome Congenital or biological problems Brain injury Foetal alcohol syndrome In-utero drug exposure Physical handicaps Genetic factors Family history of mental illness Depression Aggression Criminality Substance abuse Antisocial personality Environmental: Lack of support Absent father and extended family Isolation Lack of services Lack of care from support services Poverty Violence: victim and/or witness Multiple out-of-home placements Moves in foster care system Multiple caregivers High stress Marital conflict Family disorganization and chaos Violent community Traumatic Environment	Poor peer relationships Oppositional and defiant Demonstrates inappropriate emotional responses Lies about the obvious Lack of conscience - shows no remorse Destroys property, own or others Intense control battles, bossy and argumentative; defiant and angry Resists affection on parental terms Self destructive Lacks trust Lack of eye contact, especially with parents Manipulative - superficially charming and engaging Indiscriminately affectionate with strangers Lack of impulse control Sad, depressed and hopeless Moody, fearful and anxious Hyper-vigilant, hyperactive Learning delays Speech and language problems Negative beliefs about self, relationships, and life in general Incessant chatter and/or questions Inappropriately or excessively demanding and/or clingy Food issues - hordes, gorges, refuses to eat, eats strange things, hides food Fascinated with fire, blood, gore, weapons, evil Lack of faith, compassion, remorse, meaning Does not give or receive genuine affection and love, indiscriminately affectionate with strangers Blames others for own mistakes or problems Victimizes others or victimized Concerned about minor injuries but brushes off larger ones Parents can appear hostile and angry in some cases Child may have been neglected and/or abused in some way in the first three years of life	Unable to develop and maintain friendships Alienated Oppositional with parents, caregivers, and other authority figures Antisocial attitudes and behaviours Aggression and violence Low self-esteem Needy or clingy Reacts poorly to stress and frustration Lack of self-control Difficulty with genuine trust, intimacy and affection Negative, hopeless and pessimistic view of self, family and society Lacks empathy, compassion and remorse Behavioural and academic problems at school Perpetuate the cycle of maltreatment and attachment disorder with their own children when they reach adulthood - so it all begins again Abnormally high levels of stress hormones. This can impair the growth and development of brains and bodies resulting in behaviour disorders, depression, susceptibility to illness and difficulty learning to name but a few. RAD children are significantly also more likely to be disruptive, aggressive and antisocial.

What can I do?

Nurture

Touch is very important with children who suffer from RAD, but be sure to discuss this with parents and professionals alike, have permission and take appropriate training on how to act. Be aware of child protection issues and be sure to have another member of staff with you wherever possible – Remember you are not the child's attachment figure, you are just adding to their support.

Children with attachment disorders need to be held, so be physical, caring, and loving but also be aware that for many, touch may be associated with pain or abuse.

Make notes on how the child responds and start to learn when it is best to offer a hug and when it is best to sit back - let the child take the lead. After all, you are replacing the affection that they should have received in infancy but now they are not as susceptible to change and are self aware. Build up a relationship slowly, you have time... the more bonding experiences they have the better.

Understand

Do your research - if you understand the child's behaviours, you can use suitable behavioural and social interventions.

Example: Miss Johnson doesn't punish Joe when she finds him stealing food, why? Because she knows that Joe isn't stealing. He's horded food ever since being starved as an infant.

Imagine not knowing and punishing a child for that?

Hold regular review meetings with your child, their parents and professionals and don't be afraid to seek advice from professionals about setting boundaries and consequences – sometimes it's not the best idea and it all depends on the child. You can offer the best support when you pool your knowledge with others.

As with the attachment cycles if the trust is not there a child has no reason to think you are protecting them when you set boundaries. Why would you? They have to know you care first. By building a mutual trust, you can work on discipline and behaviour slowly.

Consider emotional age

A child with attachment disorder will often be socially or emotionally delayed, especially if they have been neglected or abused. In these cases children can often regress back to a younger age if they are upset or frustrated, so it is important to consider this when supporting them. Take a moment to evaluate where they are emotionally and act appropriately. E.g. Hold, rock and reassure them if they have regressed to age two. Comfort them with short words or sounds and pat their back.

Consistency is key

Children with attachment disorder do not usually respond well to change, so try to be as consistent, predictable and repetitive as you can. Build a routine between yourselves and stick to it so the

child feels secure and learning can take place. As the child feels safe and they open up socially and emotionally, you can then start to build the trust that has been missing from their lives.

Have realistic expectations

Abused and neglected children have so much to overcome. And, for some, they will not overcome all of their problems. It's a case of taking things one day at a time and celebrating every positive; before you know it all of the little things have grown into a happier child!

Teach by example

Introduce the RAD child to classroom routines by example. Hold a 'one-versation' with yourself and give a running commentary on what you are doing. "Now I'm going to wash my hands and dry them so I can eat my lunch". This is referred to as modelling.

Coach and care

A child with attachment disorder may have poor social skills and may need coaching during play, daily routines and interactions. As before, make suggestions rather than telling a child what to do, even if their behaviour is poor – it's a learning curve.

Help children to start building successful relationships with other children by making it clear, "If you run away with the hula hoop then the other children will probably be upset, why don't you try..." It's a huge step for the child and it takes time, but is a great goal to have.

You can also coach the child on appropriate physical behaviour as this can be an issue for children with attachment disorder. Many have little understanding when it comes to social interaction and they can sometimes frighten or shock other children with their actions. Use the 'one-versation' technique where appropriate or make suggestions rather than 'telling'.

Point out

- When it's a suitable time to groom yourself (hair, toilet, wipe nose etc).

- When and why certain behaviours are not appropriate (like touching your genitals) and when they are (washing in the bath).

- How close you are standing to people.

- When you hold eye contact and when you break it (encourage child to look at you when they are speaking – drop to their level).

- That you hug and touch people you know as you care for them. You do not show affection in that way toward

strangers as you don't know them. (Children with attachment disorder can show random affection to strangers rather than loved ones).

Be patient (and help parents and children to do the same). Parents especially can feel demoralised when improvement is slow, give yourself, parents and children a pat on the back. These things take time and you're all doing a great job!

Take care of yourself. You cannot provide the consistent, predictable, enriching, and nurturing care these children need if you are depleted; it is important to get rest and support.

More ideas

■ Make a flexible plan for each session and modify the child's workload based on their energy levels and concentration.

■ Advise the child of a safe place they can go to regain composure (away from the eyes of the class) if they become frustrated or upset.

■ Recommend any support groups for foster families/families, or find out if there's a RAD group in your area that the family may like to attend.

■ Support the child through spells of poor concentration. Offer planners for them to make notes, audio books for reading time and journals for them to log what they have done so they can remember/look back during the next session.

■ Introduce work in manageable chunks

■ Make suggestions rather than telling

the child what to do. "Why don't you go and try that?"

■ Set behaviour goals each week with an end of week reward.

■ Offer/include play and art therapies as well as relaxation time (see Therapies section for more).

■ Introduce a contact book so that parents and teachers can communicate with each other. Parents can advise you how the child's morning has gone before they arrive at school and you will know how to approach the child. Parents can also keep up with everything that has happened throughout the day.

■ Plan to alleviate boredom. Always offer a selection of 'after work' activities so if any child finishes they can choose something to do.

■ A teaching assistant/aid should be available to support the child in their work, maintain punctuality and help them to behave and engage.

■ Make notes and hold regular reviews so you can add to the child's Individual Education Plan (IEP) as they progress. Refer to their IEP throughout the day for ideas and strategies.

And finally feelings

One of the most helpful things to do when working with a child with attachment disorder is to listen - just sit, listen, and play! When you are quiet and interact with them, you will often find that they will begin to enjoy your company, open up and talk. Take advantage of this wonderful moment

and stop, relax and enjoy your time with the child. These children will sense that you are there just for them and they will appreciate how much you care.

When you feel the time is right, take a moment to talk about feelings and try some behavioural reflection. If the child has been in a confrontation for instance, reassure them and talk to them. Tell them that it's okay to feel whatever they are feeling and ask them how they think the other child feels too. Keep the conversation light as you don't want them to feel like you're lecturing and help them put their feelings into words. Give them some example phrases or use some of the techniques from the Emotional Literacy section of this book.

Selena Ledgerton
Education & Childcare Consultant/Author

See page 26 for more information on Emotional Literacy and page 17 for Art Therapy, Sensory Play and Play Therapy and Relaxation Techniques.

Publications

There are numerous online resources about Attachment Disorder, for example a handy printable guide can be found here: http://www.oaasis.co.uk/documents/Guides/Attachment_Disorder_Guide

A formal information sheet can be found here:

http://www.oaasis.co.uk/documents/Info_Sheets/Attachment_Disorder_Info_Sheet

Developing Attachment in Early Years Settings
Veronica Read
David Fulton Publishers 2009
ISBN: 978-0415491648

Parenting Other People's Children: Understanding and Repairing Reactive Attachment Disorder
John Stroller
Vantage Press 2006
ISBN: 978-0533153220

Understanding Attachment and Attachment Disorders: Theory, Evidence and Practice (Child and Adolescent Mental Health)
Vivien Prior and Danya Glaser
Jessica Kingsley Publishers 2006
ISBN: 978-1843102458

Visual impairment

The Code of Practice includes the principle that, wherever possible (and subject to parental views) children with special educational needs should be educated in mainstream settings. This includes the education of the under-fives and so we can expect to see visually impaired children in our nurseries and Reception classes.

What do we mean by visual impairment?

Visual impairment (VI) refers to those children who have difficulties in seeing which call for the use of special educational methods and adaptations to materials and who need to use specialist aids and equipment for learning. (For example, the use of low vision aids - magnifying glasses, CCTV, large print and Braille.) The term covers those children who are blind or partially sighted but not children who wear glasses. For common eye conditions such as myopia (short-sightedness), hypermetropia (long-sightedness) or astigmatism (where the eye focuses unevenly and objects are seen as blurred and distorted) then a child's vision will be corrected through wearing glasses.

Children with a VI, though, are not a heterogenous group. The children will have a range of personalities, interests and abilities as well as a range of types and degree of VI, from relatively slight loss through more severe degrees of loss to total blindness. For example, a child may experience one or more of the following:

■ Have only light perception

■ Have a blurred view of the world

■ Have only central vision and no peripheral vision (tunnel vision)

■ No central vision and therefore difficulty with colour and fine detail

■ Pain and distress caused by bright lights

Approximately 1 in 2,000 children is visually impaired. Yet children with total blindness form less than 20 per cent of the total population of children with a VI. The other 80 per cent may be registered blind but will have some useful vision. While this remaining vision may not always be very helpful to an elderly person, it has enormous significance for children who may benefit from training in interpreting the incomplete or imperfect images they see. Whatever the level of VI the child should *always* be encouraged to use their vision. Little vision does not deteriorate with use.

Specialist advisors or peripatetic teachers will support most VI children who are educated alongside their sighted peers. It will be the responsibility of this teacher to ensure that you and your colleagues feel confident in working with the child by providing practical support and advice. Parents, too, should be involved in the education of their child and can offer valuable advice on the child's specific VI, the level of their sight, what tasks present difficulties and the possible implications for learning.

Symptoms to look out for

Many of you will not have a child with a VI in your setting at the moment. However, in the course of your work you may be concerned about a particular child. What then are the possible symptoms of a VI, which may require further assessment? The list below is not exhaustive and a child may not display all the symptoms. Similarly, a child may have some of the symptoms but investigations show that they are not caused by a VI. If in doubt, observe the child over a period of time and doing a variety of tasks. Discussion with the parents should then be the first step before contacting the local authority's advisory service for VI.

Head position

■ Child moves head rather than eyes when concentrating on visual tasks

■ Frequent nodding of head when concentrating on visual tasks

■ Head tilts in what appears to be an uncomfortable position

Eye position
- Frowning or squinting when looking at pictures/books

- Aversion to bright lights

- Eyelids are drooping or swollen

- Unusual eye movements, including a rapid involuntary movement (*nystagmus*)

- Excessive blinking/rubbing of eyes

- Crossed eyes

- Closing or covering one eye when playing or working

Movement
- When walking, displays an unusual, very short, or very long length of stride

- Poor posture

- Clumsy movements, particularly prone to bumping into objects at side or at feet

- Fear of heights

- Poor balance

Behaviour
- Not answering questions unless asked by name

- Short attention span in visual tasks

- Fumbling over fine hand-eye co-ordination tasks

- Reluctance to join in outdoor activities

Effects of a VI on development
During infancy the sighted child accomplishes vast progress. They move from being egocentric to interacting sociably with peers and adults. Their language moves from babble to well constructed sentences. Their motor development moves from them having little control to that of a two-year-old who has relatively good gross motor control and is developing fine motor control. A sighted physically able child in their first few years of life seems to learn without effort - vision plays a vital role, providing a continuous, rich, consistent, precise and reliable source of information to help the child orientate to and identify objects and people.

A visual impairment imposes many restrictions on a child's ability to learn since the majority of our learning is visually based. The effects of a VI may be seen in three ways:

1. **Experiences** will be limited in range and variety - a child who does not see or sees incompletely will have a reduced ability to learn by imitation; a child who doesn't observe an activity won't attempt it for himself.

2. **Movement** may be curtailed - if there is an inability to see their surroundings, the child will be less motivated to reach out or crawl. For security the child may tend to stay in one place, thereby restricting their range of movements.

3. **Control of their environment** and self in relation to the environment is restricted. There may be a delay in bonding between mother and child due to a lack of eye contact and whereas a sighted child may smile in order to be picked up and cuddled this is lacking in a VI child. Understanding body awareness and knowing where they are in space is also hindered.

A child's play requirements will depend very much on their level of vision and visual defect. Unlike a sighted child who can use their eyes to observe the environment, a VI child will need the environment to come to them. It isn't true that the VI child will have better hearing or tactile skills and so pre-school or nursery staff must help him use these senses and make sense of a bewildering world.

How you can support the child
The five points listed here are not exhaustive but should provide a useful starting point for appropriately meeting the child's needs within the early years environment. The benefits of such a framework should in fact meet the needs of all children and not just the VI child, helping them all to make the transition between home and pre-school, between the familiar and the unfamiliar and from dependence to independence.

Partnership with parents
Nursery or pre-school may be the first time the child has left the familiarity of home for any length of time without their parents. Staff must recognise that parents know their child better than they do. The visual functioning of many VI children may vary during the day and according to their general health - it is very demanding to use impaired vision. Therefore ask the parents:

- About visual impairment.

- What is their level of sight?

- When does the child become tired?

- What tasks do they enjoy/find difficult?

- Does he wear glasses - if yes, does he also have a tinted pair?

Explain the pre-school routine carefully to parents and expect them to ask you questions. They will need this information to prepare their child.

The learning environment

Visual environment:
The lighting and decor within your setting can both hinder or help learning. Lighting does not mean bright lights - some eye conditions require lower than normal lighting levels. Blinds/curtains may be needed to prevent hard shadow and glare.

Think about the child's seating position at circle time. Do not sit/stand in front of a window - the light may cause discomfort for the child and your facial expressions will be lost.

Consider contrast within your setting - contrast between floors-walls-skirting boards, between doors and door handles (perhaps paint handles black so they are easily located). Display boards should be bright and clear and used to break up large expanses of wall. The use of colour and contrast may also enhance safety - place a dark rug on a light carpet to alert the child to the location of a piece of furniture. Provide contrasting table mats and cups to reduce spillage.

Sound environment:
All VI children will need to use information from what they hear rather more than sighted children. The sound environment should provide information to help a child understand what is happening around them and to help with orientation. Special sound clues could be introduced:

- Chimebells on the door so a child knows when someone is coming in/out.

- A whistle to signify tidy-up time.

- Goodbye song at the end of the nursery session.

As a VI child does not automatically hear better he will need to be encouraged to listen (for example, through turn taking games/sound lotto games).

Tactile environment:
The layout and organisation of the room is important. It needs to be familiar to the VI child. More than one visit prior to starting will be necessary. Actively introduce the child to the environment, telling them where they are by using landmarks. For example, talk about the rough mat by the door, the change in surface from concrete to grass when you are nearing the slide. Spend these visits, too, observing the child to see how he copes in different situations and to observe their exploratory techniques. Remember, a sighted child can continually gaze around and will gradually absorb his new surroundings, the VI child can't.

Once the child has joined your group, don't expect too much from him at first. If he is reluctant to move around then provide a 'safe corner', where he is allowed the time to explore and discover a small space which can grow as his confidence does.

The setting should be organised into defined areas: creative corner, building area and so on. Materials relating to each area should be clearly labelled and the VI child should be given plenty of opportunity to explore and handle the objects. Keep the layout the same so

he can build up a visual memory of the room and develop independence.

Presentation of tasks
This is a key issue for all children. When introducing new activities/tasks always start by using established routines and then do something new. The child must be actively introduced to environment information, for example:

- Activity areas - does the child know where they are?

- Circle time - has the child been sat in the best place to maximise visual input? Has he been shown how to do the action/finger rhymes?

- Art activities - wherever possible have a finished product so he knows what is expected.

- Snack-time - have you explained where the biscuits are kept and the milk is poured from a jug?

For close work (jigsaws, writing, threading) there should be a clear visual or physical edge to the work area so the child can easily locate the things he is using.

Where possible, toys/resources should be bold, bright and contrasting (remember - BBC). For totally blind children sound provides the only motivation to reach out and explore and so sound making toys or ones with movable parts are essential. Toys may need to be anchored within easy reach until the child has learned to search for and find them. Encourage all VI children to use both their hands, telling them what they are touching and how toys work. In this way they will begin to understand what objects are, what they do and what they feel like.

Experiences
Children with a VI need access to first-hand experiences wherever possible.

Only later in life will the VI child be able to connect the miniatures in their mind with their full size counterparts and so it is important that they handle and talk about as many manageable real things as possible. For example:

- Before setting up a laundry in the home corner visit a real laundry.

- Initially use real cups and saucers in the home corner alongside the play ones to help with association.

- Use a variety of natural objects wherever possible.

- Good quality photographs are better than cartoon pictures and do not distort a child's perception of objects.

- Think about nursery songs - does the child know what a pail is? ('Jack and Jill') Or what a spout is? ('Incy Wincy Spider').

Communication
Language is an important means of getting acquainted and sharing experiences with any child. Before the sighted child begins to speak, he is able to communicate using a number of ways. They acknowledge our presence, express preferences with a smile or a frown and understand our displeasure when we frown or can interpret our blank stares when we don't understand what they are trying to say! These non-verbal signals are completely/partly absent with a VI child who is dependent on verbal communication and physical contact. Staff will need to adopt the following strategies:

- Provide a running commentary on the world (but don't talk non-stop!) Identify objects, describe movement, for example 'I'm lifting you into the air'.

- Use relevant situational language: 'We're going into the kitchen to get the drinks tray'. In this way the child will begin to connect experiences with the words that describe them.

- At the start of new activities explain what is happening - don't assume the child will have picked up on visual clues.

- Always start a sentence with the child's name so the child knows you are talking to him.

- Always tell the child when you are approaching/leaving.

Keeva Austin, formerly manager of the Early Years Assessment Centre, Exhall Grange Special School, Coventry.

See page 26 for more information on Emotional Literacy and page 17 for Art Therapy, Sensory Play and Play Therapy and Relaxation Techniques and page 5 for Developing an Inclusive Practice.

Deafness

There are about 28,000 children in the UK with permanent deafness ranging from moderate to profound. Other children will have mild deafness and some will have a deafness that affects one ear only (unilateral deafness). Other commonly used terms to describe different types and levels of deafness are hearing loss, hard of hearing, partially deaf/hearing or hearing-impaired. Many more children will experience temporary deafness, which can be caused by glue ear. This can affect around 80 per cent of children during some stage in their childhood, so it is important that staff who work in early years settings have some knowledge of deafness so that they know how to support deaf children and their parents.

There are two main types of deafness: conductive and sensori-neural.

Conductive deafness is the most common type. Basically this means that sounds cannot pass efficiently through the outer and middle ear to the cochlea and auditory nerve. This is often caused by fluid in the middle ear (glue ear) and sometimes blockages such as wax in the ear canal.

Sensori-neural deafness, or nerve deafness as it is sometimes called, usually means that the cochlea is not processing the sound effectively. Often the cause of sensori-neural deafness is not known, but there are often hereditary factors. Deafness may be passed down in families even if there is no apparent history of deafness. Deafness can also be caused by an infectious disease such as rubella, mumps, measles or meningitis. A child may become deaf because of a shortage of oxygen in the bloodstream at birth or some other birth trauma. It is also known that premature babies are more at risk of being deaf.

When a child experiences both of these types of deafness it is often referred to as 'mixed deafness'. Few children are totally deaf. Most children will have some hearing at some frequencies.

Advice for parents

Parents who are worried about their child's level of hearing should contact their family doctor (GP) and/or health visitor (HV) and ask for a hearing assessment. The GP can examine the child's ears for any signs of infection and may prescribe a course of antibiotics, if appropriate. Some health centres can provide a hearing assessment.

Parents can, if necessary, request a referral to the ear, nose and throat (ENT) clinic or audiology department at their local hospital if they are concerned about their child's hearing and want further investigations to be carried out.

What is glue ear?

Glue ear is one of the most common childhood conditions. Children under the age of five are the largest group affected. It is a build-up of mucus or fluid within the middle ear, often associated with colds and coughs. In adults and older children any fluid produced by the cells lining the middle ear usually drains away through the Eustachian tube, which runs from the middle ear to the back of the throat. In children this tube is not as vertical and wide as it will be when they get older and as a result doesn't work as well. Glue ear is often, but not always linked with ear infections.

Treatment for glue ear

Many children may experience glue ear following a cold, which can clear without any treatment. Sometimes a course of antibiotics may be prescribed if there is any pain or sign of infection. For some children with persistent glue ear, an operation may be needed to drain the fluid from the middle ear. This involves inserting a ventilation tube called a grommet into the eardrum. This is a common treatment for glue ear and improves the hearing whilst the grommet is in place. Grommets usually stay in the eardrum until it heals and pushes the grommet out. Though an effective treatment for many children, sometimes the fluid comes back and another grommet operation may be considered.

Temporary deafness
Glue ear can sometimes develop unnoticed. Changes in behaviour, becoming tired and frustrated, lack of concentration, preferring to play alone and not responding when called may indicate glue ear. These signs can often be mistaken for stubbornness, rudeness and being naughty. Reduced hearing can make understanding conversation difficult and cause a delay in a child's speech and language development. A child with temporary deafness would still be able to hear many sounds and would generally be aware of sounds around the home. However, speech is made up of sounds with different pitches and different loudness levels that can become difficult to hear with background noise. Young children at an early stage in their language development, if affected by deafness, will have difficulty hearing all the different speech sounds and this will affect their understanding of speech, and the way they speak.

Hearing aids
There are many different types of hearing aids, some of which can transmit sounds to the ear in different ways. All hearing aids (with the exception

of cochlear implants) have a common purpose - to amplify sound. They come in various shapes and types. Most are worn behind the ear, though some are worn on the body or in the ear. Some hearing aids, such as bone-anchored hearing aids and cochlear implants, have parts that are surgically implanted into the ear. Cochlear implants, instead of amplifying sound, send electrical signals directly to the auditory nerve. The implant bypasses the damaged hair cells in the cochlea (that cannot be stimulated by conventional hearing aids) to provide a sensation of hearing.

Communication and language
The ability to develop good communication skills will help a deaf child to build up confidence to communicate with others and in turn will help them to develop emotional, personal and social skills. It is also how they learn about and understand the world around them. There are a number of factors that can help to make it easier for a deaf child to develop good communication and language skills.

These include:

- the early and accurate identification of deafness

- the family having access to clear, balanced information, advice and support

- where appropriate, access to technology such as hearing aids to make the best use of residual hearing

- positive acceptance, support and commitment from the family

- the child and family having the opportunity to learn about deaf awareness and other deaf issues

There is a range of communication options available to deaf children and their families. All deaf children have different needs, so the way in which they communicate will vary. Pre-school children will either be encouraged to develop their speech and language skills through spoken English or through sign language or a mixture of both.

Many parents will want their child to learn to speak. However, some parents might decide, either soon after their child has been identified as deaf or when it becomes obvious that their child is struggling to acquire spoken language, to introduce sign language. They will use signs taken from British Sign Language, a visual language using handshapes, facial expressions, gestures and body language to communicate. It has a structure and grammar different from that of written and spoken English. Sign Supported English uses BSL signs but in English word order. Many parents may use this at first and develop their BSL skills at a later stage to coincide with their child's language acquisition.

If a parent decides not to use sign language they will most probably use one of the auditory-oral approaches which maintains that with the use of hearing aids, cochlear implants and radio aids to amplify residual hearing, children can develop their listening skills and so a spoken language. The most widely used of this approach is the natural aural approach.

A child will use one of three main communication options when they attend school. These are: auditory-oral approach, sign bilingualism, and total communication (TC).

Communicating with a deaf child
- Make sure you have a child's attention before starting to sign or speak to them.

- Make sure there is good lighting so that your face is not in a shadow and the child can read your facial expressions and/or lipread.

- Make sure that you are facing the child and maintaining good eye contact. Don't sit too close. For lipreading and signing purposes the best distance is between 1 and 2 metres.

families to try out at home and in school. If you would like more details of the Blue Peter Loan service, or any other aspect of technology, please contact the Technology Service Team at the NDCS.

- Speak clearly, naturally and at a normal pace (speaking too slowly or shouting will distort lip patterns).

- Try to make sure that background noise is kept to a minimum. Children who use hearing aids/cochlear implants or children with mild or unilateral deafness will find it particularly difficult to pick out what is being said.

Teachers of the deaf
Very soon after a child has been identified with a permanent deafness, the family are contacted by a teacher of the deaf (often a peripatetic). Their role will be to support a child's development of language and communication skills. This will be the same whether they use oral skills, such as speech and lipreading, sign language or a combination of both of these. If appropriate, they can also support a child within a mainstream setting.

The pre-school period is a critical time for acquiring good speech and language skills. There is a constant need for repetition of speech sounds to give them adequate experience of speech and the ability to associate speech with meaning.

Technology in the classroom
Equipment such as a soundfield system is a good way of improving acoustic conditions in the classroom for all children. This system includes a microphone, worn by the teacher, which is connected to an amplifier. Loudspeakers are fitted around the classroom, often on the walls or ceiling.

Radio aids are used to help make listening in the classroom easier for children using hearing aids or cochlear implants. The teacher wears the transmitter with a microphone. The sounds are then transmitted by radio waves to the receiver, which is worn by the child. A radio aid helps to reduce the background noise and helps a child to concentrate on one person's voice, ie the teacher.

The National Deaf Children's Society loans out radio aids and other environmental aids for children and

See page 26 for more information on Emotional Literacy and page 17 for Art Therapy, Sensory Play and Play Therapy and Relaxation Techniques and page 5 for Developing an Inclusive Practice.

Autism

Take a moment to imagine what it would be like to live in a world where words, gestures, facial expressions and displays of emotion mean almost nothing to you. This is the isolating experience of more than 500,000 families in Britain whose lives are touched by autism.

What is autism?

Autism affects the way a person communicates and relates to people around them. The term autistic spectrum is often used because the condition varies; some people may have accompanying learning disabilities while others are more able, with average or above average intelligence.

Asperger syndrome is at the more able end of the spectrum while Kanner syndrome, sometimes referred to as classic autism, is at the less able end. However, despite wide-ranging differences, everyone with the condition has difficulty with social interaction, social communication and imagination.

Early signs

Parents are astute judges of their child's development and most often it is they who notice that 'something is not right', usually when their child is around two to three years old.

Distressingly, in some cases a child may seem to be developing quite normally and then suddenly appears to start losing the skills that he or she has acquired.

The signs of autism are varied. Parents and carers might notice that their child takes no interest in creative or imaginative play, preferring to repeat the same activity time and time again. Perhaps they find that their child repeats actions or words, behaves in public in ways that are odd or inappropriate, fails to make eye contact or has an almost obsessional interest in a particular subject or object - it has not been unknown for children to become fascinated by household appliances like vacuum cleaners!

In addition, a child with autism may become very distressed if routines are altered - for example, if mum varies the usual walk to the shops, or decides to serve the evening meal at a different time.

Relationships can be difficult and not only for parents. Children with autism can sometimes appear to be disruptive, rude and indifferent to other youngsters when playing or socialising. Occasionally their behaviour in public can be misunderstood by onlookers as a display of temper or naughtiness - the resulting comments made can be distressing and hurtful for parents who are doing their best to cope in a difficult situation.

Diagnosis

Early diagnosis is vital to ensure that the child and family receive support and educational guidance as soon as possible as this can have a positive impact on the future.

Most parents who suspect something is wrong approach their GP. They may also contact their local authority to ask for an assessment of their child's needs. However, although awareness of autism is increasing, some families still experience frustrating delays before their suspicions are finally confirmed and a diagnosis obtained. (Occasionally, some of the more able children with autism, including those with Asperger syndrome, are not diagnosed until they are in their mid to late teens - sometimes even later.)

Support for parents

Once a firm diagnosis is obtained, a prime question for parents is education. A key aim is to overcome or reduce the disabling effects of autism by providing a broad and relevant curriculum and giving extra help in the areas of communication and social skills as well as compensating for difficulties in imagination.

In the nursery or pre-school situation an autistic child will need specialised assistance targeting these areas and to help them cope with the school environment generally. It is accepted

that early intervention can make a real difference to the life of both the child and their family.

The National Autistic Society has a project known as EarlyBird which aims to support parents in the period between diagnosis and school placement. As part of the project, therapists work with parents to establish good practice in applying a knowledge of autism. They are shown techniques to put them in control of their child's development at an early age, to help pre-empt inappropriate behaviours and realise their child's potential.

Helpful approaches
Early years workers who care for a child with autism should be aware of several helpful approaches.

Visually interesting toys/activities: Children with autistic spectrum disorders tend to prefer toys that involve visuo-spacial skills such as shape and colour matching, jigsaw puzzles or constructional materials. Examples include: bubble blowers, torches, shape and colour matching toys, jigsaws, pop-up toys, construction toys, train toys, drawing, colouring and painting, books with flaps, touch and feel books, puzzle books and videos.

Physical activity: It is useful to encourage physical activities that are enjoyable without the need for imagination or understanding and use of language. Physical exercise is reported to diminish inappropriate behaviour and such activities are also helpful for improving motor co-ordination. Many children love 'rough and tumble' play which helps them develop eye contact and social interaction. Examples include: swings, slides, musical toys, water toys, rocking horses, trampolines, climbing frames, ride-on toys, paddling pools, sand pits.

Games to play with other people: Routine is important. Try to engage the children in simple games. Dancing games such as 'The Hokey Cokey' involve others and have consistent rules. Other examples include: pass the parcel, 'Round and round the garden', simple picture/lotto games, skittles and catch the ball games.

Appropriate provision
As a spectrum disorder, autism demands a flexible response and in practical terms a range of provision is needed. Many authorities aim for all children with special needs to be taught within their local mainstream schools. This gives the children a chance to become integrated into society with non-disabled peers and offers the possibility of making friends close to home.

General points to bear in mind

Remember that you are trying to improve the quality of life for the child, helping him or her to behave in a more socially acceptable way so that others respond better and so that the child is happier.

■ Make sure that the day is predictable and safe by establishing meaningful routines. Children with autism learn best through practical activities that are meaningful to them, for example routines for putting on clothing, eating, play.

■ Keep calm and avoid using a raised excited voice. Use gentle, slow movements with frequent smiles and touches.

■ Language - keep it simple, often backed up with photographs, pictures, body language, gesture and facial expressions.

■ For any child with autism, learning to communicate about the things that are important to them is the best place to start.

■ When trying to work with an autistic child get down to their level by sitting or kneeling on the floor, or for a more structured approach use a small table with a chair at the right height.

■ For young children with autism a key aim is to help them enjoy exploring their own lips, tongue and teeth and the sounds they can make. It is important to make any play with sounds fun.

■ Encourage children to join in with 'turn taking' play using sounds. This is a way of practising conversation as well as practising speech sounds.

■ Encourage words - but don't worry if they don't sound quite right to begin with.

■ The play of children with autism is often taken over by their need for 'sameness'. Play becomes another sort of repetitive activity which can block other people out. Try to encourage variety in the child's play so that new experience and learning is made possible.

■ Children with autism also need to learn how to play with people. They need to learn that people can be interesting and fun. Again this opens up a whole range of new experiences and opportunities to learn.

■ Keep a watchful eye to ensure that the child is not teased or bullied.

For some children with autism mainstream education is both appropriate and desirable. With the support and advice of knowledgeable professionals it can be adapted to meet individual needs. For other children, however, the mainstream environment can be terrifying and confusing with things appearing to happen at random and in unexpected ways. This leads to great distress for the child and disruption for the school.

While excellent, high quality specialist education for children with autism exists in the UK, sadly there are too few places and parents often have to struggle to find the right place for their child. Sometimes their choice is limited or the place they eventually find is many miles from home.

Kate Griffin,
National Autistic Society.

See page 26 for more information on Emotional Literacy and page 17 for Art Therapy, Sensory Play and Play Therapy and Relaxation Techniques and page 5 for Developing an Inclusive Practice.

Organisations to contact

(NAS) National Autistic Society

Full contact details for these organisations can be found on pages 87-88.

Cerebral palsy

From the moment of birth, or soon after, children with cerebral palsy (cp) have very different learning experiences from their able-bodied peers.

Babies experience a short, frustrating period of helplessness quickly followed by an increasingly active exploration of their world. They experience their world through lying, sitting, reaching, rolling, crawling and standing. In a few months they are up and away. Babies born with cp do not explore their world independently at the same times as their peers, if at all. Many, in addition to the physical difficulties, also have an altered perception of space and altered sensations of touch. The picture they build of their world may well be a very different one to others of their age.

When a small child with cp joins a pre-school group where staff have little or no previous experience to draw on staff will be unsure of their ground. They should be reassured that their experience of working with and understanding the needs of a broad range of children will stand them in good stead. However, it is important for staff to have a basic understanding of what cp is and how it affects children.

What is cerebral palsy?

Cp is caused by abnormalities in the brain usually before, during or soon after, birth. Fifteen hundred babies are affected each year, roughly one in 400 children in the UK. Cp is not infectious and, although the disability may become more noticeable with age, it is not progressive. Cerebral palsy jumbles up the messages going from the brain to the muscles causing them to behave oddly. There are three types of cerebral palsy corresponding to the three areas of the brain that can be affected.

The first is spastic cp which occurs when the part of the brain controlling thought, movement and sensation is affected. 'Spastic' means 'stiff' and the stiffness can affect the arms and legs and possibly the neck and trunk. The terms quadriplegia (four limbs),

diplegia (both legs) and hemiplegia (one side) are used to describe this type of cp. The muscles are very tight and limbs get pulled out of line.

The second type, athetoid cp, results in children having floppy muscles and uncontrolled movements of their legs and arms. When messages are sent to move muscles the floppiness can rapidly become tightness causing the limb to fly outwards. Children may also have difficulty with the fine movements of the mouth and tongue, causing problems with speech, chewing and swallowing.

The third type, ataxic cp, causes shaky, jerky movements and particularly affects fine motor control. Children with ataxia may also be unsteady when walking.

Children may have some effects and not others. Some children are only mildly affected while others are profoundly affected. Some may experience two, or all three, types of cp. There is no treatment or cure but some of the effects can be helped by therapy and teaching. Because the muscles pull abnormally they can cause the child to sit or lie in odd ways which can result in stiffness and pain. Correct positioning in sitting, standing or lying can go a long way to helping prevent pain and can really make a difference to helping the child get involved in learning.

Four out of ten babies born with cerebral palsy have other difficulties. Some children have great difficulty unscrambling the messages they receive from their eyes. In the most severe cases children may appear blind but more commonly will have difficulty making sense of pictures or writing.

Spatial awareness
Many children have difficulty with spatial awareness. If they are walking or moving their own wheelchair they bump into things; they cannot judge the speed of cars when crossing the road. In the group they may find it difficult to judge how much space they need and may 'push in'. Commonly they find it difficult to hold the picture of an object in their head with consequences for copying and mathematics.

Hearing difficulties
Hearing difficulties are commonly associated with the athetoid form of cp but colds and glue ear affect all children. Many children are sensitive to sounds and startle at loud noises. Usually they become more tolerant of noise as they become used to the group.

Speech problems
Speech problems are common. Speech and language therapists will suggest the best way to help the child communicate, and also help with chewing or swallowing problems. Most children will use speech to communicate but some will need an alternative form either to help them make their meaning clear or as their best way of talking. If children get speech aids early it can help reduce frustration. Speech aids might come in the form of a picture book or symbols, like little cartoons, that the child points to in order to clarify meaning. For some children the speech aid will be in the form of a speech synthesiser with pre-recorded messages activated by pressing switches. Using a speech aid will never prevent speech and it can help the child take part in group work and shout out with the others. Speech and language therapists will recommend what the individual child needs.

Epilepsy
Epilepsy is the additional problem most commonly associated with cp and is usually easily controlled. The medicines may affect the child's behaviour and learning and the likely effects should be recognised. Where children may have a fit in the group it is important to reassure staff by doing a thorough risk assessment and gaining confidence in how it will be handled.

Assessing the child's needs
Many youngsters with cerebral palsy have odd sleep patterns that can affect their readiness to learn. They will be frustrated by their disability and may be angry. Many children, even those with average or above average ability, will have difficulty with speaking, reading, drawing and mathematics. When the children are young it can be difficult to know whether the learning difficulty is because of ability or because of the barriers. One useful way to assess a child's needs is to spend time observing him in different situations. Watch the eyes and watch for signs of anticipation. Does he laugh at adult-to-adult humour? Does she get angry with herself when she can't complete her task? These signs will help you to gauge the level of ability.

Each child is an individual but most children will benefit from the early learning experiences provided. They will enjoy the chance to experience messy play and to be part of a larger group. Most pre-school toys will have additional uses to stimulate listening or speech. Toys that react to voice are often particularly useful, as are cause and effect toys that react to touch. Toys

that have interesting smells or textures are useful and can help staff to develop an understanding of the child's range of expressions of pleasure and dislike!

Supporting parents
In most cases the parents have already become experts on the way cp affects their child but in some cases, where the child is more mildly affected, the parents may only suspect that there are difficulties and staff may have to help them to get a diagnosis. If parents suspect that their child might have cp they should discuss it with their GP and may find it helpful to contact a local group.

Where the child has already been receiving support, parents and therapists or other carers can give a great deal of information before the child joins the group. It is vital that staff other than the child's support assistant become confident in handling, positioning and communicating with the child. A child may visit the group without this happening, a child may be made welcome, but for the child to be included everyone has to feel confident.

Lindsay Brewis,
Lead adviser, Education, Scope.

See page 26 for more information on Emotional Literacy and page 17 for Art Therapy, Sensory Play and Play Therapy and Relaxation Techniques and page 5 for Developing an Inclusive Practice.

Organisations to contact

Scope

Full contact details for these organisations can be found on pages 87-88.

Communication delay

By the time a child is three, they should have mastered all the skills necessary to communicate with the adults and children in their environment. However, studies show that approximately seven per cent of all children in the UK do not develop those skills.

What is a communication problem?

Early years workers are likely to come across children with varying degrees of impairment in communication. Broadly speaking, a speech and language impairment means that a child may have difficulty in:

- how they say their sounds;

- how much they understand what you say;

- how much they can say, that is the size of their vocabulary, how many words they can string together to form a sentence.

Types of impairment are:

- Specific language delay/disorder (differential diagnoses will be discussed later)

- Phonological delay/disorder

- Phonetic delay/disorder

- Developmental dyspraxia

The term 'impairment' includes children who have a delay or disorder. If a child has a delay, we would expect her speech and language to be similar to a child of a younger age - that means that the child is acquiring skills at a slower rate. A 'disorder' exists where skills are not being acquired within the correct/known developmental sequence. Speech and language development is different from the sequential norm.

Prevalence and causes

Speech and language impairments occur more frequently in boys than girls. It is not

always clear why a child has a speech and language impairment. He may be born with it, or could have acquired a speech and language difficulty. Apart from this, the causes aren't clear-cut. A distinction should be made between innate and environmental causes. There are, however, some at risk factors to look out for such as:

- Family history of speech delay/ disorder;

- Traumatic pregnancy and/or birth;

- Recurrent ear infections/glue ear;

- Sensory deprivation;

- Feeding/swallowing problems;

- Emotionally deprived/unstable environment;

- Limited exposure to good models of language at critical points of language development.

How speech and language impairment manifests itself

A speech or language impairment can affect a child in three ways:

- behavioural;

- educational;

- emotional.

Behaviourally, children with speech and language impairment can be withdrawn and quiet within the class environment or, alternatively, extremely active with poor concentration. They often have difficulty following adult-directed activities, for instance story time, and they tend to respond poorly to verbal instructions. There are children who remain confident speakers in spite of their difficulties; these are generally more outgoing by nature.

These children may display a number of educational characteristics:

- Make limited contributions to activities that require verbal skills, such as telling a story and during show and tell sessions;

- Have poor listening skills - instructions need to be repeated a number of times before they are able to carry them out, or they are easily distracted by noises in the classroom;

- Mispronounce words;

- They compare well with others on non-verbal tasks;

- Have limited amount of speech;

- Have limited range of vocabulary;

- Have difficulty in acquiring new words;

- Find it difficult to find appropriate words to express themselves;

- They mainly use simplified sentences, single words or sounds;

- They put words in the incorrect word order;

- Have difficulty in understanding abstract concepts such as emotions and time;

- Make consistent/inconsistent substitutions of sounds.

The emotional effects could be:

- Have difficulty when playing with their peer group;

- Become frustrated which results in temper tantrums when they can't make their needs known or when they are misunderstood;

- Poor self-esteem;

- Poor integration into their peer group.

The practitioner's role

If you suspect that a child has a speech and language impairment, the parents or carers must be informed. They, in turn, should tell their GP, health visitor or local child development clinic and ask for a referral to a speech and language therapist.

The child will need an assessment so recommendations on therapy can be made. Therapy can be given on an individual or group basis.

Liaison between the therapist and the pre-school is essential in addressing the child as a whole.

In the classroom

- Create a good listening environment by using soft furnishings to absorb sound.

- Keep comments short.

- Use as many senses as possible to aid in learning.

- Have a variety of activities available for the child who has poor attention control.

- Vary activities that are challenging, for example listening to a story, with fun and more active types of activities such as painting, outside play or musical chairs.

- Physical contact such as sitting in a worker's lap, can be a great help for children who struggle with attention control and listening.

- Use lots of animation at story time, and rather tell the story in short sentences than reading it word for word.

- Music is a powerful tool in gaining children's attention and stimulating listening and language skills by action songs, for example.

- Using a musical tone of voice can also help.

- Do not make the child talk; instead, follow their focus of attention and comment on what they're doing. The likely response is that the child will naturally want to tell you about his/her interests.

- Regular discussions with parents or carers are helpful when it comes to activities that involve talking within the group. Find out what the child's or family's interests are and when there's a special occasion in the child's life.

- Repeat the child's utterances back to him and model the correct form to him.

- Do not put the child in the spotlight, such as in show and tell activities.

- Avoid asking 'testing questions' like "What colour is this?" or "What is this?". Children with a language impairment feel tested and will naturally withdraw. When you find yourself wanting to ask a testing question, use that moment to tell the child what the answer would have been - "It's a blue truck".

Reserve time, even just a few moments per day, in a quiet and relaxed environment where you can spend quality time with the child and focus solely on *playing* with him.

Relationship with parents

A trusting relationship between parents and practitioners is invaluable. Parents are useful sources of information, to help us see and address the child's needs as best we can, taking all aspects of child development into consideration. Specific times need to be set aside to meet with parents. As children with speech and language impairment often struggle with generalisation of concepts, words and skills learned, parents need to reinforce activities at home. Speech and language impairment influences many other areas, social interaction and behaviour and parents frequently need some practical advice on how to help their child at home. Strategies are often put into place in the pre-school that can be successfully applied in the home environment.

Tania Crampton-Hayward, senior paediatric speech and language threrapist at The Speech, Language and Hearing Centre, Christopher Place, London.

Organisations to contact

Royal College of Speech and Language Therapists

Afasic Unlocking Speech and Language

The Association of Speech and Language Therapists (ALSTIP)

The Speech, Language and Hearing Centre

Your local authority

Full contact details for these organisations can be found on pages 87-88.

See page 26 for more information on Emotional Literacy and page 17 for Art Therapy, Sensory Play and Play Therapy and Relaxation Techniques and page 5 for Developing an Inclusive Practice.

A stammer

Speech is a skill which develops rapidly during a child's first two years as he learns to make meaningful sounds and words. We often take for granted that a child will learn to talk easily and freely but, like learning to walk, there will be bumps, stoppages and starts, before children learn to co-ordinate all the necessary skills and talk smoothly.

Although all children repeat words and phrases, pause between words with 'ums' and 'ers', and often hesitate, some children will stammer and have more difficulty than others in learning to talk smoothly. There has been a commonly held belief that young children who stammer simply grow out of the problem if it is ignored. However, stammering is a complex problem and parents often wonder if the stammer will get worse, whether they should do something, and if so, what help they should seek.

What is known about stammering?

Five per cent of all children under five stammer and just over one per cent of school age children stammer. Stammering occurs in all cultures and social groups and affects four times more boys than girls (therefore this text uses 'he' instead of 'she'). It most commonly begins between the ages of two and five years old - the average age of onset is 32 months. Fortunately, most of these children will not continue to stammer into school age, but around two in five are likely to continue to stammer unless they receive help early from a speech and language therapist.

It is not known why young children begin to stammer but it is recognised that a combination of factors is involved. In about 60 per cent of cases, there is a family history of stammering, or other speech and language problems in one or more relatives. However, other factors can affect a child's ability to speak fluently, including their language and motor skills, environmental, social, emotional, and psychological factors.

How will you know if a child is stammering?

If you look after a child who is stammering there are several things which you may notice:

- that the child's speech does not seem to flow smoothly - it may sound tense and jerky;

- the child is putting extra effort into saying his words;

- the child is aware that he is finding talking difficult or shows signs of being frustrated;

- that the child gives up talking half way through a sentence or a story.

Or you may hear the child do one or more of the following things:

- repeat parts of words and whole words; for example "Ca-ca-ca-can I have a drink?" or "I-I-I-I want a story";

- lengthen sounds; for example, –"He is sssssssssitting on the chair";

- block - this is where the child knows what he wants to say but gets stuck on a particular word; for example "Where's . . . . daddy gone?"

Stammering varies a great deal from child to child so you may hear some or all of these things when the child is talking.

One of the features of early stammering is that it tends to come and go. Children can often have days, weeks or months when their speech seems to flow easily and smoothly and the stammer seems to have disappeared, and other times when the stammering is more noticeable and the child finds talking difficult again. Even within one day you may notice that a child's stammering varies:

■ it may be more obvious when he is feeling tired, unwell, excited, or anxious;

■ it may change depending on who he is talking to, for example other children, adults, carers or strangers;

■ or according to the situation, for example if it is noisy, quiet, rushed or relaxed.

What should you do?

Because you are with the child regularly you hear him speak at different times of the day and in different situations, for example when he is playing alone or in a group, first thing in the morning or when he is more awake, so you are in an ideal position to notice if a child is stammering or finds talking difficult.

If you think a child you look after is stammering the first thing to do is to discuss this with his parents or carers. If stammering is identified and treated early enough, therapy is effective and can help the child overcome the stammering. Therefore if a parent/carer is concerned in any way it is important that they do not delay in asking for a referral to their local NHS speech and language therapy (SLT) service either through their health visitor or GP, or directly, by contacting the SLT department.

Practical ways of helping

There are many things you can do to help a child who stammers talk more easily.

■ Listen and respond to what the child wants to say not how he says it.

■ Don't look away from the child when he stammers.

■ Be patient and allow the child time to complete his thoughts and to speak rather than finishing the child's sentences or interrupting him.

■ Reduce the number of questions you ask, and make sure you give the child

time to answer one before asking another.

■ Slow down your own rate of speech slightly - this is more helpful than asking the child to slow down or to stop and start again. Slowing down helps the child feel less rushed when they talk.

■ Pause before answering a child who stammers as this makes the conversation feel less hurried.

■ Praise and encourage the child for what he does well. This helps build confidence.

■ When it comes to behaviour/ discipline treat every child the same.

Children who stammer require your full attention when they're communicating and respond well to a structured environment, routine and a less hurried lifestyle.

If the child needs to tell you something, give him your full attention.

Where to go for more help

If you suspect a child you look after is stammering, it is important that his parents or carers seek professional help from a speech and language therapist (SLT) as soon as they become concerned - preferably from an SLT who specialises in stammering. Stammering can be prevented from developing if it is treated

early enough. Parents and professionals can contact the British Stammering Association's Information and Counselling Service to receive a free information pack, details of their local NHS speech and language therapist service and whom to contact to make a referral.

Elaine Christie
is a specialist speech and language therapist working in private practice in London and Kent. Before that she managed an early identification project at the British Stammering Association.

See pages 17-25 for further information on Art Therapy, Sensory Play and Play Therapy and Relaxation Techniques and page 5 for Developing an Inclusive Practice.

Organisations to contact

The British Stammering Association

Full contact details for these organisations can be found on pages 87-88.

Down's syndrome

The human body is made up of cells. Each cell is like a tiny factory, which makes the materials needed for growth and maintenance of the body. Contained within each cell is a set of 46 chromosomes (23 pairs), half of which come from the person's mother and half from the father. The chromosomes carry the genes that are inherited from a person's parents.

What is Down's syndrome?

Down's syndrome is a condition that occurs at or around the time a baby is conceived. Most people with Down's syndrome have an extra copy of chromosome 21 in every cell, making 47 in all. It is not yet known what causes this to happen. However, it is something that occurs in all races and all social classes. It is known that the chance of having a baby with Down's syndrome is higher in older mothers, although, because more babies overall are born to mothers in the 25- to 30-year-old age group, the majority of babies with Down's syndrome are born to 25- to 30-year-old women. We do know that, in the vast majority of cases, Down's syndrome is not passed down from generation to generation.

The presence of the extra chromosome has the effect of disrupting the growth and development of the baby. Quite how much effect the extra chromosome has varies from person to person, although all people who have Down's syndrome have a certain degree of learning disability.

People with Down's syndrome are as different from each other as any other unrelated members of the population. Like the rest of us, they get all their genes from their parents, so they look and act much more like members of their family than someone else with Down's syndrome. Their abilities and skills, strengths and weaknesses are just as variable as they are amongst the rest of us.

It is important not to make generalisations about people with Down's syndrome, but to look at each person as an individual.

How common is Down's syndrome?

In every 1,000 live births, one baby will be born with Down's syndrome. That is about 600 babies every year in the UK.

Diagnosis

In most cases, it becomes clear quite soon after birth that the baby has Down's syndrome. Doctors and midwives are usually alerted by certain signs that are more common among babies with Down's syndrome than among other babies. For example, if doctors detect a heart disorder it may alert them to the possibility of Down's syndrome because about 40 per cent of babies with Down's syndrome also have a heart problem. Diagnosis can be confirmed by a blood test to analyse the chromosomes.

It is important to stress that it is not possible to tell how disabled a child will be at this early stage. The number of physical characteristics of Down's syndrome a child has bears no relation to his or her degree of developmental delay.

Developmental delay

For a variety of reasons, such as poor health and/ or hospitalisation at an early age, some young children with Down's syndrome will be more delayed than others. By the time children reach three or four, it may be apparent that they are not as advanced as their ordinary peers. Nowadays, most young children with Down's syndrome will have benefited from an early intervention programme (sometimes known as Portage) designed to help them gain the skills that other children learn naturally. Such programmes can be encouraging to parents who feel they can be actively involved in promoting their child's development. An early intervention worker will help parents to teach their child by breaking down tasks into small manageable steps. In some areas of the country, Portage is available from the age of six months; in others it starts later.

Speech and language delay

Speech and language difficulties are common in young children with Down's syndrome. Most children will be under

the care of a speech and language therapist who will give parents and carers (including early years workers) guidelines on how to encourage the speech and language development of the child according to an individual programme.

Common health problems

Children's development can be delayed because of health problems that are more common in Down's syndrome.

Hearing

Many children with Down's syndrome have hearing problems caused by a condition called glue ear, which can be a consequence of repeated upper respiratory infections such as colds, or infected or enlarged adenoids. The fluid in the ear becomes thick like jelly and cannot drain away and hearing is affected. This can happen in all children but it is more frequent in children with Down's syndrome. Glue ear can cause deafness, infection, pain, delayed speech development, and temporary behaviour problems. Glue ear can be successfully treated, but early years workers need to be aware that the effects of hearing impairment can be reduced by a few simple steps outlined below:

- Always give the child plenty of time to respond to anything you have said - they will get frustrated if you start saying something new before they have had time to respond to the first thing you said. (This applies to most children with Down's syndrome whether or not they have any degree of hearing loss.)

- Try to face the child when speaking to them.

- Don't shout but speak clearly.

- If the child does not understand, don't just repeat what has been said but try to rephrase it.

- Make sure the child is paying attention before you start speaking.

- Give the child lots of visual clues - signs and gestures - to help them understand what you are saying.

- Keep your hands and any visual aids away from your mouth.

- Don't use exaggerated lip movements.

Vision problems

Some young children with Down's syndrome need glasses to correct their vision and, just as with other children who wear glasses, you may need to make sure that the child does wear them when necessary.

Lack of muscle tone

Many babies with Down's syndrome have poor muscle tone and tend to be 'floppy'. In most cases, this improves as the child grows. However, it can contribute to delay in learning how to run, skip, throw and catch (gross motor skills) and affect the development of skills such as writing (fine motor development). Most children will master these skills eventually, but may take longer than their peers to do so. Many young children with Down's syndrome will have regular physiotherapy sessions either at home or at a child development centre. These sessions are designed to give parents exercises to do with their children to help them achieve particular skills.

Monitoring development

The developmental progress of children with Down's syndrome will usually be monitored by staff at the local child development centre. In the early years, parents are often offered extra support by a specialist health visitor or a social worker who is able to keep them informed of facilities for children with special needs in the area.

How to cope with questions about difference

Pre-school children in general tend to accept differences in colour, behaviour and so on much more readily than older children might. Most of the time, if children in a group ask questions about a child being different, it will be enough to point out that we are all different - 'You have blonde hair but Jessica has black hair'. The Down's Syndrome Association (see box) has a list of recommended reading books for children which deal with issues of difference.

Relationships with parents/carers

Most parents of a child with Down's syndrome will have become experts on their child's condition and needs. They need to feel that their views and knowledge are being respected and taken into account. Communication is the key to successful inclusion and many potential problems can be avoided by both parties keeping the other informed. It may be helpful to remember that a child with Down's syndrome is a child first and foremost and that his or her condition is secondary.

Sarah Rutter,
Information Manager,
The Down's Syndrome Association.

See page 26 for more information on Emotional Literacy and page 17 for Art Therapy, Sensory Play and Play Therapy and Relaxation Techniques and page 5 for Developing an Inclusive Practice.

Organisations to contact

Your Local Authority

The Down's Syndrome Association
The Down's Syndrome Association has an information service and also a number of advisers it can call on for specific information about such things as speech therapy, medical and behaviour problems.

Attention deficit hyperactivity disorder

Research suggests that attention deficit hyperactivity disorder or ADHD is genetic and bio-neurological in origin, but there are still those who claim it is an excuse for parents and teachers who cannot cope with normal, albeit challenging, children. The use of medication to treat ADHD is also controversial: is it a mind-altering drug used to control children for our own convenience or an effective treatment for a neurological impairment?

Having reviewed the research on ADHD, the British College of Psychiatrists stated, in their publication *FOCUS: On the Use of Stimulants in Children with ADHD*, that we should see the disorder as a threshold which can be reached by a combination of inherited, social and psychological factors. This helps to explain why there is a high family incidence of ADHD, affecting five to nine times as many males than females. Estimates of prevalence vary between two and five per cent, but if the same rates, using the same criteria, assess a group of children for ADHD the number is fairly constant across all ability levels, cultures, and classes.

There are three types of ADHD:

■ children who are predominantly hyperactive and impulsive;

■ children who are predominantly inattentive;

■ children who have AD and HD combined and are both hyperactive/impulsive and inattentive.

Common characteristics
Parents and teachers typically describe the first and last of these two groups in the following way: driven by a motor, restless, fidgety, volatile, attention seeking, unable to sit still, unable to listen, distractible, quickly bored, demanding, bossy, accident prone, 'in your face' and highly impulsive - acting first and thinking second. The children usually have problems with waiting and turn-taking - in conversation, games and queues - and find it almost impossible to raise a hand rather than shouting out. The ADHD toddler can seem unkind: pushing another child out of the way, snatching a preferred toy and sometimes acting aggressively. Attempts to control the child frequently result in a temper tantrum.

Conversely, children who have the inattentive version of ADHD are often dreamy, under-active, ambivalent children who are easily overlooked by their peers and at risk for learning difficulties. More girls than boys fall into this category, which affects less children than the other forms of ADHD.

I will focus on the more common forms of ADHD (hyperactive/impulsive and combined). At a psychological level, the core problem for these children is poor self-control. Areas of the pre-frontal lobes - the part of the brain that deals with self-management - are under active and, as a result, it is hard for the children to control their activity level, behaviour and mood. These problematic behaviours have an early onset and are persistent over time and across settings. However, children with ADHD can have distinctly good and bad days and nearly always behave well in a clinic where they enjoy the novelty and attention. This raises an important fact about ADHD: these children do not have problems concentrating on favoured activities. In fact the opposite is true: because it takes self-control to stop doing something you enjoy it can be much harder for a child with ADHD to stop watching TV or playing with his video than it is for his non-ADHD sibling or classmate.

Diagnosing ADHD
Diagnosing ADHD is exceptionally difficult for several reasons. Firstly, many other disorders present with similar or overlapping symptoms, and more than half of the children with ADHD have other areas of difficulty. Secondly, ADHD is not a categorical condition, such as a broken leg which is either broken or not broken, but a continuum disorder where the cut-off point is not always clear. Thirdly, environmental factors, such as a disruption in attachment, can sometimes cloud the issue. Lastly, there is no test for ADHD: diagnosis depends upon clinical judgement, which is why multi-agency assessment is all important.

Because the prognosis for many children with ADHD is not good - many of them go on to have social, vocational and relationship problems - early identification is critically important.

Supporting children with ADHD
The recent and highly important Multi-Modal Treatment of Attention deficit hyperactivity disorder study, conducted by the American National Institute of Mental Health, showed that stimulant medication is the most effective way of managing the core ADHD symptoms (although other, associated behaviours, also require behaviour management), but medication is not recommended for children

under the age of six, and many parents understandably do not want to go down this route. It is hard work to support a child with ADHD without medication, but it can be done! If you suspect you have a child with ADHD in your pre-school group or class, here are some suggestions.

Firstly, discuss the problems with the child's parent/s or caregivers (in practise usually the mother). Be careful not to use negative language such as 'naughty' or 'bad' that will make the mother feel she is being judged as a poor parent. Start off with positives, describing the child as lively rather than hyperactive, full of enthusiasm rather than impulsive. Never discuss the child while he is present, in front of other parents or in a public place such as the playground.

Before you see the parent, write out a list of problems and then use the 'Three basket' method. In the first basket put the problems that are harmful or illegal: running out of the playground or hurting other children. In the second basket put the problems that seriously annoy you such as constant shouting. In the third basket put everything else. Now accept that you can only tackle one or two problems at a time, choose the problems from the first basket, and only discuss these problems with the mother. This will counter feelings of helplessness, give you a realistic chance of success and the confidence to tackle new targets.

Make a plan. The target must be realistic or both you and the child will fail. It must also be clear and simple so that the child understands exactly what you mean. For example, if you ask a child to be 'kind' he will argue relentlessly when you say he has not been kind. Be explicit: being kind involves no biting, thumping, pinching or hitting. Use circle time to discuss what we mean by kindness, and at the start of each day give every child five smiley faces. If they are unkind they lose a face: if they are extra kind or helpful to another child they can win a face back. At the end of the day, children with three faces have a certificate to take home.

Research has shown that this method, which is called 'response cost', is particularly effective with children who have ADHD. These children need immediate rewards, and are better if they start with the reward than if they work towards it. It also means that a child can win back all they have lost, and this is particularly important for children with ADHD as they give up easily.

In addition to this specific plan, here are some other strategies which research shows are effective:

■ Try to have a calm, organised classroom with an established daily routine. Warn the child well ahead of any changes, such as a new helper, and prepare the child for changes of activity: 'We'll be packing up in ten minutes, five minutes - I'll put the cooker timer on so that you can see how much time you have left'.

■ Try to ignore minor naughtiness and be sure to praise the child - even for something small - at least three times each day. Be quick and generous with praise.

■ When a child is naughty, make sure he knows you like him but not his behaviour.

■ Make sure the other children know you like the child. Social rejection is a major problem for children with ADHD, and we know that it has an early onset and is slow to turn around. It is also true that children who are popular with their teacher are more likely to be popular with their peers.

■ Never resort to anger, ridicule or sarcasm. This will inflame the situation and have a lasting effect on the child.

■ Never get involved in an argument: this is highly rewarding to children with ADHD. Simply state, in a relaxed, calm voice: "You know the rules, it's your choice" and then remove your attention. It is difficult to do, but effective!

■ When faced with a melt-down tantrum give the child an opportunity to calm down and save face by saying: "OK, you can play for another five minutes". After five minutes the child will often back down and you can then discuss the matter. This has been found to be much more effective and less disruptive than trying to insist on immediate compliance.

■ Avoid confrontation by giving the child choices. For example, when he refuses to draw a picture ask: "Do you want to draw with felt-tips or crayons?", or "Do you want to finish your picture before drink time or after?"

■ Try to make eye contact with the child when you are talking to him.

■ Have a home/school diary so that you are in constant touch with the parents.

■ Adopt a whole-school approach and support one another.

Remember that if you can help a child with ADHD in these formative years you are significantly improving his chances of a happy, successful life. If the problems prove intractable, this in itself is valuable evidence that should be passed on to the school educational psychologist or medical officer.

Jenny Lyon,
specialist educational psychologist.

Please note that 'he' rather than 'she/he' is used throughout as the majority of children with ADHD are male.

See page 26 for more information on Emotional Literacy and pages 17-25 for Art Therapy, Sensory Play and Play Therapy and Relaxation Techniques and page 5 for Managing Behaviour.

Organisations to contact

ADDISS - ADHD Information Service

Full contact details for these organisations can be found on pages 87-88.

Publications

Multi-Modal Treatment of Attention Deficit/Hyperactivity Disorder (MTA study). Numerous papers have been published about this study. Details can be found on the following website: www.devdis.com

Royal College of Psychiatrists' Research Unit, 1999, *FOCUS on the Use of Stimulants in Children with AD/HD*

Information about AD/HD and other developmental disorders, contacts for family support groups, recommended books, videos and training can all be found on the following website: www.devdis.com.

Dyslexia

In the past, it was thought children could only be diagnosed as dyslexic from the age of six. It is now evident that there are many signs well before school age. Parents and pre-school carers and educators are in the strongest position to recognise those signs, and to provide the right activities to help.

The word 'dyslexia' was originally coined from the Greek and, taken literally, means 'difficulty with words'. The old way of describing it was 'word blindness' – an inability to read letters and numbers in the right order. However, that's far from the whole picture.

Dyslexia is best described as a combination of abilities and difficulties which affect the learning process in one or more of reading, spelling, writing and sometimes numeracy.

Accompanying weaknesses may be identified in areas of speed of processing, short-term memory, sequencing, auditory and/or visual perception, spoken language and motor skills.

Some children have outstanding creative skills, others have strong oral skills. While not every dyslexic child will be outstandingly talented, all have their own strengths.

Dyslexia occurs despite normal intellectual ability and conventional teaching. It is independent of socio-economic or language background.

Britain has two million severely dyslexic individuals, equivalent to four per cent of the population. This figure includes around 375,000 schoolchildren. A further three million people have dyslexia in its mild or moderate forms.

This means that it affects about ten per cent of the population, either directly or indirectly. Put another way, 20 per cent of all children with special educational needs will be dyslexic. It is vital that such children's abilities and difficulties are identified as early as possible and that the right teaching provision is put in place.

Early signs
A child's behaviour may be an early indicator of learning differences. It can range from diffidence and a lack of self-esteem to the other extreme – being cocky and acting the class clown.

In addition, a pre-school child who is potentially dyslexic may:

- Know colours but confuse them – for example saying 'black' instead of 'brown'

- Have an early lisp

- Struggle to remember the label for known objects – for example table, chair

- Confuse directional words like up/down, in/out

- Find it hard to learn nursery rhymes or even rhyming words

- Have a problem with sequences – for example coloured beads – and later with things like days of the week or numbers

Possible causes
Experts don't always agree on where the exact cause of dyslexia lies. Researchers

at Sheffield University have found that the cerebellum area of the brain, which controls movement – anything from riding a bicycle to threading a needle, doesn't function as well as it should in dyslexic people.

Dr John Stein of Oxford University points out that dyslexics often have difficulties with precise movements – and the eye movements needed for reading are extraordinarily precise. His research indicates that dyslexic people have a problem measuring the timing of messages from both the eyes and the ears.

Most researchers into causes of dyslexia are looking at the area of the brain affecting language. Most dyslexic people, even when good readers, have continuing difficulties with phonological awareness – recognising sounds and analysing small parts of speech. Many experience some difficulties with speaking words – thinking of the right word for an object, muddling words, for example by saying par cark instead of car park or rapid naming, for example quickly saying ten animals beginning with 's'.

Supporting the dyslexic child
These activities will benefit the whole pre-school group not just those children who may be dyslexic.

- Say nursery rhymes together

- Read poetry to children, especially amusing or nonsense verse. Try making up jingles or limericks

- Mime a particular nursery rhyme or incident and encourage the children to guess the rhyme. They can then choose something to rhyme in return

- Use drama

- Provide pictures to talk about, using prepositions in discussion: 'Is the man in the blue hat in front of or behind the lady?'

- Play 'Simon says' – starting with simple instructions but gradually making them more difficult – for example 'Simon says touch your ear and your nose then clap your hands'

- Board games like snakes and ladders, Ludo and bingo help develop turn-taking

- Joining dots, mazes and simple picture crosswords can all be useful

- Clap words of one syllable before

moving on to two-syllable words, then more. Say the words as you clap them – for example tel – e – vi – sion

- Use songs involving memory and sequencing – for example 'Old Macdonald had a farm'

- 'I went to market and I bought...' – start groups that are easy to remember, for example fruit and veg, then introduce a more random list

- Say a group of words with a 'stranger' in it – for example 'cat', 'dog', 'apple', 'fox'. The child draws a picture of the stranger. Ask why it is different

Relationships with parents
For some parents, it may be a relief that someone else has picked up on their child's difficulties. They may have noticed problems but not voiced them or they may have attempted to express their feelings and met with comments like 'Don't worry. Don't expect too much. He will catch up.' At worst, the parent may have been labelled fussy, pushy or overanxious.

Building a strong partnership with parents is vital. Bear in mind that dyslexic difficulties can be extremely sensitive and it is important to broach the subject with sympathy and tact. A mother, in particular, is often perceptive about her own child. Her comments should always be listened to, and her concerns taken seriously.

Remember to emphasise the positive aspects of dyslexia and that it is common. Today, dyslexia is viewed as a combination of abilities as well as difficulties. Dyslexic people may have good problem-solving skills, enhanced creativity and excel in the arts, design, architecture and computing. Stress

that, with the right intervention and support at this early stage in the child's education, there is no reason why he or she should not thrive.

Where to get help
During regular pre-school development checks, a doctor or health visitor may see children with an uneven development profile, indicating weaker areas which need attention from a speech or language therapist and/or an occupational therapist to look at fine motor co-ordination problems, and/or a paediatric physiotherapist for gross motor problems.

It is helpful if information from all these sources, along with parents' and pre-school educators' comments, are made available to the headteacher when the child enters his first school. The valuable observations and record-keeping of parents and early years educators can prevent the situation where it takes several years for a child to be identified as dyslexic, by which time failure and consequent behavioural problems may well be all too apparent.

Juliet England,
British Dyslexia Association.

See page 26 for more information on Emotional Literacy, page 15 for Portage and pages 17-25 for Art Therapy, Sensory Play and Play Therapy and Relaxation Techniques and page 5 for Developing an Inclusive Practice.

Organisations to contact
The British Dyslexia Association

Full contact details for these organisations can be found on pages 87-88.

Dyspraxia or developmental coordination disorder (DCD)

Until ten to fifteen years ago the term dyspraxia, meaning a deficit in movement planning, hadn't been heard of in the UK. Children with motor coordination difficulties would probably have just been thought of as clumsy.

Dyspraxia - also known as developmental coordination disorder or DCD - is about ten years behind in terms of its acknowledgement and research in comparison to dyslexia. It is part of a spectrum of specific learning difficulties along with AD/HD (attention deficit/ hyperactivity disorder), Asperger's syndrome and dyslexia. It affects between four and six per cent of the population and about three times as many boys as girls.

What causes DCD?

There has been little research completed looking at the causes of developmental coordination disorder. There are both environmental and genetic factors at play. This means that often someone else in the family may have had dyslexia or other learning difficulties but when they were growing up they may not have been recognised.

Is the incidence of DCD on the increase?

More children are now being identified as having dyspraxia and this may be due to an increase in the condition because of different parenting styles today.

How have parenting styles changed?

The 'Back to sleep' campaign now encourages parents to place babies on their back for the majority of the time. In the past, they would have put babies to sleep in prams or cots during the day and placed them prone as well as on their backs.

Nowadays, most babies are usually either in a car seat, which is carried in and out from the car, and placed on the floor, or in a pushchair. In both cases the child is supine (on the back) rather than in a

prone (on the front) position. Children are not placed on a baby mat on the floor as often as they used to for fear of it being dirty. The use of playpens has also been limited as they are now seen as trapping the baby, rather than allowing them to explore their environment safely.

For most babies, these changes won't have a long-term affect. However, for the low -toned, floppy child, the opportunity to gain greater head and shoulder control and hip stability is essential for future development. The floppy baby is also likely to cry when placed prone, as he is not able to lift his head for any length of time. This, combined with changes in parenting styles, may be the reason why there is a growing incidence of non-crawlers as well as more cases of DCD being identified.

The prone position is important as it allows the child to strengthen the neck muscles, do push-ups (ready for crawling) and learn to reach for toys (helping hand- eye coordination and bilateral integration).

The child with DCD may also walk later and for this reason may be put in a baby walker. Yet the child with DCD often has poor hip stability and the modern baby walker tends to make them sit down rather than use it as a support. He then moves around not just in a forward direction but also sideways like a crab! The older style walker with bricks in it made the child stand up to hold on to the bar in a good walking style.

Children with DCD also often have sequencing and rhythm problems that affect them in games and with activities like writing and mathematics. Early games played at home such as singing nursery rhymes, catching and throwing balls are less common as children turn to television and video for entertainment, even at a young age.

Fewer children are eating together with families at mealtimes and this means that they are not getting the chance to practise key skills such as using cutlery (helps bilateral integration skills - a

pre-cursor for writing) and sitting at the table and taking turns (helping, listening and social skills).

Children's diets have also changed. Today we eat more processed foods and less fish regularly. There is growing evidence that fatty acid supplements such as cod liver oil or Eye-Q (available over the counter at chemists) are especially helpful because it is thought that some children with dyspraxia have problems metabolising certain fatty acids needed for brain and eye activity.

How would you recognise a child that may have dyspraxia?

- Late motor milestones - this means that the child may have been later sitting, crawling, walking or talking. Some children may not have crawled at all.

- Balance problems – the child may be unreasonably afraid or conversely unaware of danger in precarious situations. Climbing on a climbing frame or along a wall or walking downstairs may make the child very nervous. The child may also be unstable if not sat properly in a chair with their feet on the floor.

- Poor bilateral integration – the child may find it difficult to coordinate both sides of the body. This may make using a knife and fork or handwriting harder to do.

- He may seem to run in a rather ungainly manner, may need to use his arms to help balance, and find that stopping is quite hard to do. Catching and throwing a ball may be harder to do, as well as being able to stand on one leg, skip or jump.

- Younger children often find a bicycle is harder to pedal.

Fine motor skills

- Immature grasp and poor dexterity – there may be difficulty holding and manipulating small objects, for example doing up buttons, holding and using a pencil, using scissors and playing with jigsaws.

- Poorly established dominance – the child may not seem to be clearly right- or left-handed. He may use whichever hand is nearer to reach.

- The child may have poor pencil control, and find drawing and colouring in harder to do than his peers.

Learning difficulties
The child with DCD may experience difficulties with:

- Letter and shape recognition.

- Writing - their writing may vary in size and quality from the top of the page to the bottom. The letters may go above and below lines on the page. (Even at the age of seven or eight the child may still have writing that looks more like a four- or five-year-old's.)

- Counting and recognising numbers.

Language and communication
- The child may have been slower to acquire clear speech and may still have poor speech which may be less distinct when the child is tired.

- The child may not join in with other children, playing alongside rather than interacting with them.

- He may appear at times not to be listening.

Behaviour and emotion
- Distractible – the child may appear to be distractible but this may be because of his inability to balance on a chair or filter out unwanted sounds, movement or a visually busy environment.

- Frustration – this usually presents for the younger child with behaviour which is better in school than at home. The child may have tantrums even as he gets older, especially at home.

So what can be done?
If you suspect that a child may have dyspraxia, early recognition and prevention is better than intervention. Therapy will help some children if their symptoms are more severe but plenty of play experiences to build up muscle control are important. For the younger child, the best advice is to encourage big play, such as setting up obstacle courses, playing on the floor and swimming. Give them a big paintbrush and a bucket of water and let them 'paint' the walls or fence outside.

Make sure the child has their basic building block skills in place before moving onto more complicated work. The child with DCD often seems younger and just needs a bit of extra time to learn new skills.

They should see their GP or health visitor who could refer them on to a children's centre for a full assessment.

For parents, one of the most important things is to be kept informed of what help and support their child is receiving in your setting and who they should liaise with (SENCO or class teacher) and where they can get further advice through the education authority and local support groups.

Dr Amanda Kirby,
Medical Director, The Dyscovery Centre,
Cardiff.

See page 26 for more information on Emotional Literacy, page 68 for Working with Children with Learning Difficulties and pages 17-25 for Art Therapy, Sensory Play and Play Therapy and Relaxation Techniques and page 5 for Developing an Inclusive Practice.

Organisations to contact

The parents' first port of call should be their GP or health visitor.

Dyscovery Centre
The Dyscovery Centre assesses and treats children with dyspraxia and supports their families but can also help with information for teachers. The centre provides awareness days and has a one-stop shop for toys and equipment.

The Dyspraxia Foundation
The Dyspraxia Foundation is a national charity promoting the awareness and understanding of dyspraxia. It publishes information, organises conferences and has local groups across the UK.

Full contact details for these organisations can be found on pages 87-88.

Obsessive compulsive disorder

Most children like to follow routines, brushing their hair and teeth, or storytime with Daddy and tucked in by Mummy – it provides security and stability.

The warning lights begin to flash when a child insists on performing time-consuming and seemingly purposeless rituals, such as washing and re-washing hands after touching a toy or checking and re-checking a desk to check everything is 'just so' before they leave. Such behaviours may indicate that a child is suffering from obsessive-compulsive disorder, or OCD.

What is OCD?

People with OCD suffer from intrusive, unwanted and sometimes upsetting thoughts that they just can not escape (obsessions). They then feel compelled to repeatedly perform ritualistic behaviours and routines (compulsions) to try and ease their anxiety.

As many as 1 in 100 children may suffer from OCD. The peak age for diagnosis of OCD in children is ten years old, although it can strike children as young as two or three.

The distressing thing about this disorder

is that children with OCD cannot help what they are doing and in severe cases can even cause themselves pain by their own compulsions. Children have been known to wash their hands until they are red raw for example. Obsessions and compulsions can also take up a great deal of time and be most upsetting. Many children will begin to develop complex rituals and may count or check things repeatedly to ward off unwelcome thoughts and feelings. Some children live in constant fear of doing something wrong, that they may lose something in error, or hurt somebody.

Michael: "If I turn these light on and off ten times and those pencils line up in all the same colours then nothing bad will happen when I go outside".

Children with OCD feel powerless to stop their thoughts and behaviours. They may be unaware that their actions are irrational or unusual and may wish to defend what they are doing. On the other hand when compulsions become too much, children with OCD can feel isolated when others shy away from them, seeing their routines as strange.

Children can become upset by the amount of disruption their OCD causes. Obsessions and rituals can interfere substantially with everyday routines and schoolwork, family and social activities can all be affected. Children can also begin to have temper tantrums if their compulsions are interrupted as they know have to start again – another compulsion. It's a vicious circle.

Common Obsessions:
- A need for symmetry and order

- Fear of contamination or germs, along with a washing compulsion such as hand washing.

- Fear of harm or danger to a loved one or self (i.e., if I count to seven every time I speak to my mum, she won't die)

- A need for perfection (i.e. re-drawing a whole picture instead of

erasing a mistake, re-positioning everything so that things are just so)

- Fear of losing something valuable

- Intrusive words or sounds

- Aggressive or sexual thoughts

- Religious fixations

Common compulsions:
- Counting or touching rituals (i.e. tapping everything in the room or in a specific order and making a noise or counting as they do so)

- Taking, hoarding or saving useless items

- Seeking reassurance or doing things until they seem perfect

- Washing and rewashing hands to avoid exposure to germs

- Arranging or ordering objects in a very specific way

- Repeating a name, phrase or tune

- Asking the same questions over and over again

- Missing out specific numbers when counting

- Avoiding using scissors or anything that could cause harm

- Checking lights are off or that doors are locked repeatedly

Signs of OCD:
It can be difficult to recognize symptoms of OCD in children, as some may go to great lengths to hide their behaviours.

Symptoms can start with something simple; a child may begin to line up their pens or toys perfectly for example. But all it takes is a strange glance from a passing child to make them feel 'different' and from then on they'll perform these rituals alone.

Children may also try to resist their obsessions and compulsions at school but not at home, or vice versa.

Unfortunately, the consequence of this secrecy is that children with OCD can go undiagnosed for long periods and miss out on professional help until years after the onset of their disease.

By that time, they may have learned to work their lives around the rituals.

Common signs of OCD:
- An obsessive fear of germs or mess (relating to germs)

- Rough, red hands from incessant washing

- A sudden increase in laundry

- An inordinately long time spent completing homework

- Holes erased through tests or homework

- A sudden drop in school performance

- Pleads with family members to repeat phrases over and over again

- Recurrent fears that something bad will happen to a family member or other loved one

- Extreme distress or tantrums if a ritual is interrupted

- Difficulty concentrating at school due to repetitive and intrusive thoughts

- Social isolation or withdrawal from peers

How does OCD affect a child?
OCD can affect:

- A child's success at school

- Never ending obsessions and compulsions may make it difficult to concentrate in class and complete homework

- Personal relationships with family and peers. Strange behaviours may result in teasing from other students, and both siblings and parents can become frustrated, sad or exasperated with OCD rituals and the disruptions they create

- Physical health. As well as other anxiety disorders, children with OCD

can suffer from physical, stress-related symptoms, such as headaches, hair pulling and stomach aches.

As with many of these disorders, symptoms can worsen during times of stress.

What causes OCD?
OCD is somewhat of a mystery as no-one knows conclusively what causes it.

Research has shown that OCD is a brain disorder caused by a chemical (serotonin) imbalance and that environmental and genetic factors may also play a role.

The disorder appears to run in families, so a child of one or two parents with OCD may be more likely to develop it.

OCD is not caused by stress, though the loss of a parent or similar stressful event can trigger the disorder.

How is OCD diagnosed?
A medical health professional will examine the child and discuss their symptoms with them. They will collect information from home, school, parents and professionals and make a diagnosis (including a treatment plan).

A child will usually be diagnosed OCD if their obsessions and compulsions take over at least one hour of their day and disrupt their normal function. (This is the same for adults.)

If you suspect a child in your care has OCD or any anxiety disorder then you should inform your line manager and refer the child's parents to their doctor. Their GP will then refer them to an appropriate mental health professional for diagnosis and treatment.

Treatment
There are currently three beneficial treatments for OCD:

Cognitive Behavioural Therapy (CBT)
After making the child aware of their problem, a clinician will discuss their OCD obsessions and compulsions. They will then help the child try alternative actions which focus on positive thinking and positive behaviour patterns (as

Exposure and Response Therapy (ERP)

This is a type of Cognitive Behaviour Therapy where a child will be prevented from performing OCD rituals for a short amount of time; this period is increased with each session. Although this therapy can cause anxiety in the beginning, these feelings quickly decrease when a child understands what is happening (and feels the benefits).

A typical course of ERP treatment may take 10 to 15 weeks and a child will usually have a weekly review with their mental health professional while these are taking place.

Medication

Medication is sometimes used alongside Cognitive Behaviour Therapy. Seek medical advice and research all medications to be aware of frequency, dosage, adverse or allergic reactions and side effects.

Associated disorders and issues

Some children with OCD can suffer from other disorders as well, including Tourette's syndrome, attention deficit hyperactivity disorder (ADHD), depression, social anxiety, and panic disorder.

If a child appears to have problems at school after OCD symptoms are treated, you should consider having them evaluated for learning disabilities and other disorders.

How can I help?

It is important to let children know that their OCD is not their fault. Many children respond well to the idea that the OCD is a bit of a bully who's trying to take over.

OCD-UK is one of the leading charities for OCD and the organisation is run by sufferers themselves. They have produced a fantastic information leaflet for children depicting the 'OCD Bully'. Not only is it filled with fantastic advice, but it is great for you and the child in your care to read regularly together.

Other ways to help include:

- Listening to the child's feelings.

- They can give you the greatest insight into their condition.

- Recognising and praising small accomplishments. When living with OCD symptoms a child may have poor self-esteem, a low tolerance for frustration, a depressed mood and temper outbursts, and may well blame others when things go wrong. None of these are a good starting point for a recovery plan where the child is the one making the effort, so the more you can do to build their self esteem early on the better. (See Emotional Literacy & Therapies Section for more).

- Modifying expectations as symptoms wax and wane. If you see that your child is struggling with their symptoms, allow a few more minutes to complete the set task.

- Measuring progress on the basis of individual improvement not OCD statistics or class standards. How have things changed for the better since last month, last week or yesterday? Any improvement is a positive.

- Being flexible and trying to maintain a normal routine. You should also have a support system in place for yourself as caring for a child with OCD can be stressful and tiring. Have someone to talk to and be sure to take any set breaks; you'll perform so much better when you are calm and positive.

A positive note: If you've had a bad day, remember that all anxiety

disorders are treatable, and that with proper treatment by a mental health professional, children with OCD can go on to live full and productive lives. You are contributing to this, you should be very proud.

Selena Ledgerton
Education & Childcare Consultant/Author

See page 15 for more information on Portage, page 68 for Working with Children with Learning Difficulties and pages 17-25 for Art Therapy, Sensory Play and Play Therapy and Relaxation Techniques and page 5 for Developing an Inclusive Practice.

Organisations to contact

OCD-UK
OCD-UK is a leading charity for people who are affected by Obsessive-Compulsive Disorder (OCD) and is run by sufferers for sufferers.

Full contact details for these organisations can be found on pages 87-88.

Tourettes

The onset of Tourettes syndrome occurs at around 5-9 years of age on average, however it's important to include here, as symptoms such as tics and snorting can begin from age 3. The earlier these are noticed the better the chance of appropriate support and treatment.

In 1973 there were only 485 recorded cases of Tourettes worldwide and yet today the syndrome is identified in between 6 and 10 children per thousand, meaning up to 106,000* children aged 5–18 years may have Tourettes in the UK – many of these children go undiagnosed as their symptoms go unnoticed or are mild and cause no stress or issue.

*Stern JS, Burza S, Robertson MM. "Gilles de la Tourette's syndrome and its impact in the UK". *Postgraduate Medicine Journal*. 2005 Jan; 81(951):12–9

Tics

A tic is an involuntary and rapid recurring action. Tics consist of repetitive or sequential movements and can be simple or appear co-ordinated.

Tics are the most noticeable characteristic in children with this disorder and they can present themselves in various forms.

Simple motor tics can be fast and random whilst complex tics are slower and can appear deliberate. Vocal tics follow a similar pattern.

In the public eye, involuntary swearing is the most familiar symptom connected with this disorder. Yet Coprolalia is rare in young children and only occurs in 10 to 30 percent of adults*. It is important to know that this symptom does not have to be present for Tourettes to be diagnosed.

*Robertson, M.M. "Annotation: Gilles de la Tourette syndrome-an update." *Journal of Child Psychology and Psychiatry and Allied Disciplines* 35/4 (1994): 597-611

Below is a tbale showing the different types of tics and their symptoms.

Pattern?

There are no patterns to these tics and although their occurrence can be rare when a child is young, they can increase to over 80 times per minute in extreme cases (sometimes more).

Tourettes sufferers can experience periods where they are tic free for a length of time and some children experience less tics when they are concentrating on a task and more when they relax afterward. This can also happen if a child is tired, pressured or stressed – different times, changing severity and alternating frequency, this is referred to as 'waning and waxing'.

A child can present one or more of these tics, though neck and head tics are the most common. It is good to be familiar

with them all and make notes of any you see. You should discuss these with your line manager (in a confidential setting) and ensure that parents, practitioners and professionals are aware of anything new.

Should you work in a residential post or be planning an overnight trip with your setting, research has shown that tics also occur throughout sleep. If your child has aggressive/severe tics you should take appropriate care/protection equipment for overnight and discuss the child's night routine with parents.

WARNING: Be aware of choking/ strangulation hazards during overnight care – bibs, wipes, cushions, bolsters, comforters etc.

Simple Motor Tics	Complex Motor Tics	Simple Vocal Tics	Complex Vocal Tics
Abdominal tensing	Copropraxia (obscene gestures)	Using or repeating sounds such as 'oo' 'uh' 'ee' 'boo'	Muttering
Arching (of the back), twisting or tensing	Echopraxia (imitating the movements of others)	Sucking sounds	Changes in breathing pattern
Kicking	Kissing	Coughing	Altering speed of speech
Eye blinking	Licking	Sniffing	Animal noises
Finger flicks/movements	Spitting	Spitting	Repeating phrases 'Uh-Oh', 'Shut up', 'You Know', 'Okay'
Mouth opening	Facial gestures	Throat clearing	Stammering
Tongue protrusion	Head banging	Snorting	Change in tone, rhythm, volume or accent
Eye rolling	Pinching	Screeching	Repeating phrases or words until they 'sound right'.
Jaw snapping	Rubbing	Screaming	
Teeth clicking	Hopping	Whistling	Palilalia (echoing the spoken word)
Facial grimacing	Biting lip	Clicking	
Nose twitching	Gyrating	Grunting	Coprolalia (involuntary swearing, shouting, speaking)
Lip pouting	Touching objects	Barking	
Shoulder shrugging	Bending	Clacking of the tongue	
Arm jerking	Twirling		
Head jerking			
Head nodding			
Jerking any part of the body			
Knuckle cracking			
Frowning			

Medication

Neuroleptics and other medications can be highly effective in suppressing tics, but adverse side effects can limit their usefulness and use on very young children is rare.

If your child is prescribed medication for their condition, discuss this with parents and professionals involved. Research the specific medication and be aware of the frequency and dosage as well as all possible side-effects.

As always, store medications safe and securely as per your settings policy.

If you are advised that a child is trialling different dosages to see what works for them, be aware that in some cases medications can produce different symptoms or make current symptoms more severe. Children can also have allergic or adverse reactions. Seek medical advice before caring for a child trialling medication.

Other Characteristics

As well as the symptoms above, children can demonstrate other characteristics.

Transient Tics: Transient tics can appear in numerous areas, though they are normally found on the face or neck and can last weeks or months (usually no more than a year). Different tics can occur in this way over several years; they

normally appear between the ages of 3 and 10 and are more common in boys.

Chronic Tics: Chronic tics are found on the face or neck and do not tend to vary. They last longer than a year and can include neck jerks, blinking or facial expressions.

Children with Tourettes may also have:

- Some form of attention deficit
- Some form of obsessive-compulsive behaviour
- Ritualistic behaviour
- Repetitive behaviour (usually until something is 'perfect' or 'just so')
- Some form of learning difficulties/disabilities
- Disconnected aggression (without inhibition or fear of consequence) in the form of breaking things, kicking, punching or shoving for example.

You're a hero!

All of these behaviours are part of the syndrome and not purposeful or deliberate. It is important to be resilient, keep a positive attitude and not think that negative or aggressive behaviours are directed at you – it's nothing personal, you are appreciated.

So what can I do?

Understand the condition – learn as much as you can about the condition so you can provide the best possible care and support. This will be invaluable when planning activities and adapting them so as to include the child. If the child's condition has just been diagnosed then you can help both child and parents through the statementing process and beyond.

Make sure that the child has access to all available professionals who can help – speech and language therapists, occupational therapists, physiotherapists, medical specialists and an art or play/sensory play therapist for example. If the child is not currently benefiting from these individuals, do a little research and provide a contact number or URL so the family can find someone appropriate (or recommend/contact someone from your own list).

Don't panic! Be aware that tics are out of the control of the person with tourettes and make others (and the other children) aware so they don't become upset or fearful – answer questions the other children ask, the more knowledge they have the less confusing the condition.

Put yourself in the place of the child – think about how you would feel.

Imagine being asked to wait while a teacher visits each table in the classroom and you can't help screaming when you become frustrated, you push everything from the table but have no control over it. The other children steer clear of you as you sometimes lash out and although you have some physical aids, you can rarely take part as adaptations aren't made to the session to include you or you become frustrated waiting for help and begin to tic. You wouldn't mind so much, but your tics ease off when you're concentrating on a task – if only you could get to take part in one!

If your child requires one-on-one help for an activity and it's not available don't do the activity. (...and have a notebook of possible activities on standby just in case).

Encourage a stress free environment – stress, anxiety, fear and excitement can all cause a child to tic. Behavioural self-management strategies tend to be used on older children but for children in their early years the emphasis is on understanding the child, minimising stress and encouraging relaxation.

Physical and emotional relaxation can really help as well as art and sensory play therapy. (See the Therapies section for some adaptable ideas.)

Make any physical adaptations required - e.g. ramps, swings, hoists, cushions, bolsters, wipes etc.

And most importantly...

DON'T GO IT ALONE – with numerous symptoms, children with tourettes are susceptible to psychological distress, low self-esteem, frustration and social anxiety so build a team and imagine your child leading it - concentrate on their needs.

Rather than your child visiting physiotherapists, occupational therapists, specialists and speech language therapists in isolation, make yourself a member your child's 'team' and invite parents and other professionals to do the same. Keep in touch and keep up to date with each other. You'll know what is happening with your child's condition from every angle, you'll know how they're progressing but most importantly you'll get to know them – you'll have a lot more to talk about!

Pay special attention to learning as much about your child as possible, their likes, and dislikes, their reactions and behaviours, everything from what triggers their frustration to what makes them laugh! Show an interest in them as a person.

It's simple to put physical adaptations in place like a ramp for a wheelchair, but not so easy to make social and instructional adaptations. Knowing your child builds a foundation for this. If a child doesn't feel emotionally understood, socially accepted and included then the physical support means nothing, both need to be nurtured.

For instance:

1. Taking time to check that one-on-one help is available means you don't have to ask your child to wait during the session and in turn cause frustration. Plan sessions carefully considering their emotional needs as well as their physical ones.

2. You can't understand why your child tics more during relaxation time when they should be calm. After trying every relaxation technique in the book you finally talk to your child a nd discover that it's nothing to do with the session – they love it! It's just that they connect relaxation time to home time (as it's just beforehand) and they're excited to see their mum.

3. As you're now part of a team, your child's parents inform you that they went to the zoo at the weekend. When your child is frustrated later and starts to tic, you help them relax by talking about the animals.

Children with tourettes can be misunderstood and frustrated. Know your child, fill your toolkit and build their self esteem.

Selena Ledgerton
Education & Childcare Consultant/Author

See Contacts Section for more information, page 26 for more information on Emotional Literacy, page 68 for Working with Children with Learning Difficulties and pages 17-25 for Art Therapy, Sensory Play and Play Therapy and Relaxation Techniques and page 5 for Developing an Inclusive Practice.

Further Resources

Tourettes Action UK
Southbank House,
Black Prince Road, London, SE1 7SJ
Tel: 0845 458 1252
Website:
www.tourettes-action.org.uk

*Tics and Tourette Syndrome:
A Handbook for Parents and
Professionals*
Isobel Heyman
and Uttom Chowdhury
Jessica Kingsley Publishers 2004
ISBN: 978-1843102038

*Hi I'm Adam: A Child's Book
about Tourette Syndrome*
Adam Buehrens
Hope Press 1990
ISBN: 978-1878267290

Learning difficulties

As more pre-school age children with special educational needs are being educated in mainstream settings, the need for information and practical ideas is becoming greater among early years professionals.

Assuming a child has no other primary cause of SEN, for example, hearing impairment, Down's syndrome or cerebral palsy, it is likely that learning difficulties will be the most common problem to become obvious at this stage.

There is no blueprint for supporting and managing children with learning difficulties. Each set of problems is as unique as the child himself. There are so many variables to be taken into account when planning a programme of work - his learning style, your teaching style, the amount of parental support, the available resources and equipment, the setting's SEN policy and so on - that each programme can be planned only by the people who will be implementing it for the child who will be using it.

Most early years professionals are excellent at identifying quickly a child who seems to be having learning difficulties. But a vague feeling that something is wrong has to be focused into specifics and then acted on. The first step in doing this is to decide whether the child:

- scores poorly on assessment tests or profiles (whether standardised tests or the setting's own admission baseline assessments) in comparison with his peers;

- has levels of development (in all or specific areas) and play that are noticeably lower than those of his peers;

- makes little or no progress despite involvement in the nursery curriculum and fails to achieve the targets set;

- makes little or no progress despite involvement in a differentiated curriculum.

If the child seems to meet all or most of these criteria, then action needs to be taken.

Steps to follow after identifying concerns

1 Involve the child's parents. This is crucial (and a legal obligation) at all stages. A positive and active relationship with the child's parents is beneficial to everybody concerned.

2 Involve the Special Educational Needs Co-ordinator (SENCO).

3 Initiate Early Years Action with an Individual Education Plan (IEP), which should include the following points:

Child's name and date of birth

Date IEP implemented

Areas of difficulty

Two or three (no more!)

Areas of work and target dates

Teaching methods

Staff involved

Frequency of programme

Criteria for success

Equipment/apparatus

Date of next review

4 Review Early Years Action and the IEP about three months after implementation. If there

are still concerns after two or three reviews, then

5 Initiate Early Years Action Plus, involving appropriate outside agents and specialist support. Review the IEP and plan a new one if necessary.

6 Review Early Years Action Plus and IEP. If there are still concerns after two or three reviews, the team will decide whether a statutory assessment is necessary.

Working with the child on an Individual Education Plan (IEP)

■ The record sheet designed by the setting should contain details of the dates that the child's performance was checked, by whom and with what result. Careful record-keeping is crucial.

■ It is also essential to make a note of which areas are giving him difficulty.

■ The Code of Practice recommends that the child's progress is reviewed every three months - it is important to keep an eye on him throughout that period.

■ The IEP can be changed at any time.

■ Be aware of the records of results - is a pattern emerging? For example, does Joe always fail to meet his targets in the same sessions?

■ The teaching methods may play a part. For example, does Joe work better in a one-to-one situation? Is there a clash of personalities with Mrs Jones? Do his sessions happen at a good time? Are the rewards and incentives offered to Joe sufficient to motivate him?

Positive teaching methods are essential

■ Always involve the child in his own record keeping. For example, allow him to put stickers on his chart or to choose which activity he wants to do as a reward for trying or achievement.

■ Always work in small steps and don't overload the child. An IEP is not fixed in tablets of stone and can be changed if the targets are too difficult for the child.

■ Always be patient. If it's a bad day and the child is driving you mad, take time away from each other and try again later when both of you feel calmer.

■ Always be consistent in your approach. This is essential for the child to be able to learn and practise the skill being taught.

■ Always give the child plenty of repetition. He'll need lots of practice and help, so don't be afraid of 'overkill'. If possible, though, try to offer different activities to consolidate the skill.

■ Always praise the child whenever he achieves success and always refer to failure in a positive way. For example, 'That was a really good try, Joe. Let's see if you can make it this time by doing ... '

■ Always be prepared to be flexible. If it takes standing on your head to get a point across, then do it!

■ Always check previous achievements on a regular basis. Skills that were taught some weeks beforehand may need to be revisited and consolidated again! Don't assume that when a target has been achieved that's the end – keep checking.

■ Always remember the child is not here for the professional - the professional is here for the child!

Collette Drifte is a writer, lecturer, INSET provider and consultant on special educational needs and early years education.

See page 26 for more information on Emotional Literacy and pages 17-25 for Art Therapy, Sensory Play and Play Therapy and Relaxation Techniques and page 5 for Developing an Inclusive Practice.

Publications

Code of Practice on the Identification of Special Educational Needs (DFE, 1994).

Excellence for all Children - Meeting Special Educational Needs (DfEE, 1997).

SEN Code of Practice on the Identification and Assessment of Pupils with Special Educational Needs and SEN Thresholds: Good Practice Guidance on Identification and Provision for Pupils with Special Educational Needs (consultation document) (DfEE, 2000).

Handbook for Pre-School SEN Provision **Chris Spencer and Kate Schnelling** (David Fulton, 1998).

Special Needs in the Early Years **Sue Roffey** (David Fulton, 1999).

SEN Code of Practice - http://www.teachernet.gov.uk/_doc/3724/SENCodeOfPractice.pdf

Existing policies

Newly appointed SENCOs should find that their setting already has a special needs policy. In this situation, it is good practice to conduct an audit. A good starting point would be to assess the success of your existing policy in terms of supporting the children with special educational needs in your setting. All staff members should be involved in this. Assess how effective the policy is in practice by giving thought to the following areas:

The effectiveness of the systems in place for admission of all children, including those with special educational needs

The systems in place for the identification of special educational needs

- How accurate are these?

- Are staff confident and aware?

- Current provision for children with special educational needs.

- How effective are the Individual Education Plans in supporting children?

- Is the graduated approach being used correctly?

- Have reviews taken place? If so, have parents and other specialists been consulted/attended?

- How effective is the curriculum offered and systems of planning for differentiating needs of all children?

Systems for observation and assessment of attainment and progress for all children

- Are these used and adapted to support the learning of children with differing needs?

Relationships with specialists and other agencies

- What links have been developed and how successful are these in practice?

Partnership with parents

- How involved are they and how happy do they seem, both with the service offered and with their child's progress?

Effectiveness of staff training

- Have staff attended relevant training? If so, how has this benefited them and the setting?

- Has knowledge gained been shared to improve understanding and practice?

Complaints procedure

- Have any complaints been received about any area of the special

educational needs provision? If so, did the systems in place support a successful outcome?

If after carrying out this process, you and your staff team are confident that your policy is effective in providing for the needs of children with special educational needs within your setting, you do not need to produce a new policy. However, you may need to update it to fulfil the requirements of the Code of Practice and to continue the process of monitoring and reviewing.

Sue Fisher,
early years training consultant.

Record keeping, planning and assessment

Record keeping is an important part of working with young children and all the more so when working with children with special educational needs.

The revised Code of Practice states that monitoring individual children's progress throughout the Early Years Foundation Stage is essential. It is the responsibility of each setting to decide the exact procedures to adopt and paperwork to use. The crucial factor is that it should support everyone in offering the best quality provision to each child.

Whilst Individual Education Plans are important for children already identified as having special educational needs, the system you adopt for assessment of attainment and progress is valuable in recording information on all children's progress and may help in providing evidence that a child is experiencing difficulties in learning. It should also provide a guide to how suitable your provision is for children with special educational needs through the progress they make.

Using a familiar system is likely to help staff feel more confident. However, as SENCO, you may feel that a new system should be put into place. If so, make sure this is positive, reflecting achievement rather that highlighting what the child cannot do.

This can be achieved for most children by breaking learning objectives down into small steps and recording the achievement of each step rather than just the overall objective. Questionnaires to parents should support assessments and help to provide a starting point for working with the child. Remember, too, that these records should include regular information on progress from parents and from other organisations involved to produce an overall picture of the child and their achievements.

Be Aware of Confidentiality:

The revised SEN Code of Practice (4.28) directs all SENCO's to Section 14 of the SEN Toolkit with regard to care and protection of 'sensitive' documents. Section 14 states that "confidentiality about certain issues must be considered". In line with the Data Protection Act 1998 be aware that documents such as IEPs, statements, assessment sheets and Child Information Records can contain personal and medical information.

All documents relating to a child should be:

- treated sensitively

- not left around

- stored securely

- not removed from the setting without the SENCO's permission

- shredded when finished with (after required archiving period)

All staff involved with such documents should be briefed/ trained on Data Protection and how sensitive or confidential documents should be stored/signed in or out.

Involving children

It is good practice to involve all children in the assessment of their progress. Children enjoy talking about what they have achieved and looking at examples of their work and photographic evidence, particularly if they appear in them! All these things encourage a sense of pride in their achievements.

How you involve children is a matter for you and your colleagues to decide but systems are most valuable and enjoyable when they are child centred and play based.

The importance of observation

Staff should be encouraged to carry out regular observations of the children in a range of situations and activities. For children with IEPs, these may be linked to particular targets. Through these observations, staff will be able to keep written notes of progress towards these targets. These can be brief bullet point notes but, kept regularly, they will provide valuable information which can be brought forward at the next review of the child's progress. If a target is not met, these notes may also help to highlight why.

Additional records to consider

Occasionally, staff members may raise a concern about a child's development or behaviour. In this case it is worth considering using an 'expression of concern' format to record written observations on the child (see page 61). This will provide useful evidence if you feel the child needs to have their needs met through Early Years Action or to support staff in providing more successfully for the child through a differentiated curriculum.

You will need to share record keeping responsibilities with staff. An additional record you may wish to keep could take the form of a diary sheet in date order to record brief details of all formal and informal meetings with parents and other professionals supporting the child, telephone calls and any other relevant information. This will provide an 'at a glance' check on decisions made.

Planning and organisation

Encourage staff to use their observations of children to involve them in planning. Through observing children at play, staff will be able to assess what children enjoy most and are most interested in as well as what fails to stimulate their interest. This knowledge and that gained from discussion with parents and other relevant people will help staff to plan around children's interests. Encourage staff to have high expectations and yet to pitch activities at just the right level for success. This will help build confidence and self-esteem.

Providing an inclusive environment

Early years practitioners will recognise the importance of making everyone feel included, settled and secure.

As SENCO, you can support staff in providing an inclusive environment through:

- providing teaching materials and books which cater for a wide range of abilities;

- talking to children about special educational needs - what it means and the forms it can take;

- helping children to think about and care for others;

- providing opportunities for each child to feel included and valued, such as through circle time activities.

- supporting children to develop positive attitudes through being a good role model;

- involving parents in children's learning and developing strong links with home;

- using teaching strategies which ensure all children are able to participate in activities (with modification, if necessary and individual approaches);

- showing realistic, consistent expectations for children's behaviour;

- using additional support if available to encourage children to join in and benefit from being part of a group.

Staff training

An important part of the SENCO's role is to provide training for other staff members. At first, it is likely that you will cover such areas as SEN awareness and inclusion, identification and assessment of special educational needs, the Code of Practice recommendations and requirements and special needs policy.

Additional training needs will become apparent from time to time, particularly when a member of staff is working with a child who has a specific condition or difficulty. You will need to support this member of staff by providing relevant information and helping to organise specialist training.

Your Early Years Development and Childcare Partnership may produce a local handbook or directory. Alternatively, you could contact local colleges, health authorities or training providers for details of relevant training. It is worth collating all information on training opportunities sent to you even if you do not feel it is relevant at the time. You will then know who to contact if the need does arise in the future.

The contacts you have made with other professionals through working with children with special educational needs

Resources for an inclusive environment

Think about the resources you provide for all the children. It is not always necessary to provide extra specialist resources - most good quality resources will be suitable.

When assessing the suitability of resources for any children, remember to consider:

- Safety

- Durability

- Attractiveness

- Suitability for purpose

Children with special educational needs will benefit from an environment which encourages sensory exploration and investigation. With a little imagination, it is easy to provide opportunities through developing the use of basic materials and activities. For example:

- Adding rice, lentils, cornflour, rose water, and so on, to playdough

- Varying the texture of sand

- Adding ice, jelly, cooked/ uncooked spaghetti to water

- Providing feely boxes, mats and displays with different materials/ textures

Many other activities you provide, such as circle time, songs and rhymes and story time, may not need additional resources. It is important, however, that you continually assess individual needs in group activities. You may need, for example, to provide crash mats under climbing equipment for children with poor balance or coordination.

Constantly observing and assessing each situation will help to ensure that you resource appropriately and provide for the individual needs of all the children.

will also prove a valuable resource in providing information or offering training.

Sue Fisher,
early years training consultant.

Statutory assessment and statements

There will be a small number of children for whom the support you give through Early Years Action Plus will not be effective enough to enable the child to make satisfactory progress. If it is considered that the child has long-term needs, the local authority may consider carrying out a statutory assessment leading to a statement of special educational needs. However, this will only be the case for no more than two per cent of children.

As SENCO, if you, in consultation with the child's teacher/key worker, their parents and other professionals involved, feel they would benefit from a statutory assessment you will be able to request this. Likewise parents or other professionals involved with the child are also able to make a referral. Statutory assessments are multi-disciplinary, in other words, they involve everyone working with the child. So, regardless of who makes the initial request, you will be contacted for your opinions.

Asking for an assessment

Your local education authority should have a named person to contact if you are considering asking for a statutory assessment. The LA will be able to tell you who to contact and how. Who carries out this role will depend on how your LA is organised. They will be able to give you advice on the process, supply the relevant forms and explain how to fill them in.

The type of information you will be asked for will include details of the child's difficulties and needs, what action has been taken to date and strategies employed, probably through Early Years Action and Early Years Action Plus, and details of any outside advice obtained and support received. It is important that you provide all this information so that the LA can seek advice from the appropriate people.

In determining whether a statutory assessment is necessary, the LA will

consider all the information supplied, and in particular:

- The difficulties you have identified;

- The strategies you have put in place through Early Years Action and Early Years Action Plus;

- Parents' views;

- Opinions and information from outside agencies.

The LA must make an assessment of all this information within six weeks and decide whether they feel they have enough evidence to carry out a statutory assessment. They will only do so if they feel that the child's needs are only

likely to be fully addressed through a statement of special educational needs. The key to this decision is usually based on whether these needs are seen as long-term needs that are likely to continue to require attention throughout all or most of their school life.

If the LA decides to proceed with the statement they will contact you again for more information. A draft statement will then be issued, followed by the final statement. The whole process must be completed within six months.

What happens if a request is refused?

If a request is refused, the LA must contact the person who made the

request and explain, in writing, why the decision was made. If you continue to feel that the child is not making satisfactory progress, you can contact the LA again after the next review of the child's IEP. If, after receiving further reports, the LA agrees that the child does require extra support, they will write a statement for that child. Briefly, this will contain:

- Details of the child's needs

- The additional help they need

- How this will be monitored

For most children, it will be possible to provide this additional help in the setting with support from your LA. Your setting will then be named in the statement and the LA will fund the additional provision specified in the statement.

You will need to make sure that you inform staff of the content of the statement and how it is to be implemented.

How might a statement support a child?

The type of additional support likely to be detailed in a statement includes the involvement of a support worker to provide:

- additional one-to-one support;

- individualised support;

- support with planning;

- support in developing IEPs and reviewing progress.

In some cases, the statement may specify additional equipment to support the child and help them to access the full curriculum and activities.

It is a misconception that additional support hours are always provided as the LA will decide upon the most appropriate support to meet the child's needs.

Statement reviews

When children move out of the Early Years Foundation Stage, their statements will be reviewed annually. The early years, however, is a time of rapid growth, development and change, so reviews should be carried out six monthly to ensure the provision being made is still appropriate to the child's needs. A statement can be amended after a six

monthly review to reflect significant changes if necessary.

As SENCO, it is likely that you will take the lead in organising the review, which can be timed to coincide with the child's IEP review. The timescale above (see box) can be used as a guide to organising and carrying out reviews.

A statement can be a valuable aid to progress for a child with special educational needs during the early years. It should provide additional support for the child at this stage as well as helping them prepare for school and making sure the child's needs are provided for during their school years.

Supporting Children & Parents through the Assessment Process:

Both children and parents should be supported when assessing for special educational needs.

Consider using discussion and explanatory leaflets for parents to encourage their participation and make them aware of the processes to come.

With regards to the child, sit down at their level and offer them a chance to ask questions. Give them as much reassurance as you can and if they have trouble understanding break the process down into manageable chunks or draw it out in steps. How about acting out meetings using puppets to put a child at ease first...

It can be a very scary time, so be sure to offer support and information throughout.

As detailed in the SEN Code of Practice, the child will soon be one of the main contributors to their own Individual Education Plan – they know themselves best and can tell you a lot. Start building that important trust now...

You should recommend any organisations/services you think may be of help and LAs should also ensure that parents are offered the full range of parent partnership services as described in Chapter 2 of the SEN Code of Practice.

Sue Fisher,
early years training consultant.

For more information on the role of the SENCO see page 2.

Suggested timescale

Before the review

Six weeks
- Invite parents, support staff, key workers and outside professionals involved with the child to attend.

Two weeks
- Request any written reports from professionals involved with the child to be submitted by this date.

- Send copies of these reports to all invited parties.

The review meeting
It is likely that you, the SENCO, will chair the meeting.

After the review
The information gathered should be collated on to a special review form (provided by the LA) and sent to the LA and all parties involved in the review.

The review form will ask whether there are any significant changes in the child's development and needs, whether the statement is still required and what the main targets for the child are. After reviewing the statement, it is still important to set out these targets in a new IEP. The review form should then be sent to the LA who will circulate it with reports and copies of the new IEP attached.

On the way...

Is a child starting at your setting with provision already in place? Want to know more? For Special Educational Provision for children under compulsory school age, please consult the SEN Code of Practice Section 4.39 – 4.53.

SEN Code of Practice:
http://www.teachernet.gov.uk/_doc/3724/SENCodeOfPractice.pdf

Early years action and action plus

The revised Code of Practice states that settings should adopt a graduated approach to providing specific help for individual children.

Your setting will already be providing a differentiated curriculum to meet the needs of most of the children you work with each day. If you feel it is necessary to provide additional or different types of support to a particular child, you should consider meeting their needs through Early Years Action.

As SENCO, it is important to remind staff that children progress at different rates and to consider what is reasonable to expect an individual child to achieve. Through working with that child, observing and assessing their progress, staff will be alerted to individual difficulties. In these cases, additional or different action will need to be taken to help the child to progress.

If parents are unaware of what is happening, the setting is best placed to judge how to tell parents that their child is receiving special educational provision because their child has SEN. Parents should be informed of the process and encouraged to contribute their knowledge and understanding of their child, and raise any concerns they may have.

Parents should always be consulted and kept informed of the action taken to help the child, and of the outcome of this action.

The SEN Code of Practice defines adequate progress as progress that:

- closes the attainment gap between the child and the child's peers

- prevents the attainment gap growing wider

- is similar to that of peers starting from the same attainment baseline, but less than that of the majority of peers

- matches or betters the child's previous rate of progress

- ensures access to the full curriculum

- demonstrates an improvement in self-help, social or personal skills

- demonstrates improvements in the pupil's behaviour

The code also identifies triggers for intervention through Early Years Action when children are making little or no progress.

Despite receiving appropriate early education the child:

- makes little or no progress even when teaching approaches are particularly targeted to improve the child's identified area of weakness

- continues working at levels significantly below those expected for children of a similar age in certain areas

- presents persistent emotional and/or behavioural difficulties, which are not ameliorated by the behaviour management techniques usually employed in the setting

- has sensory or physical problems, and continues to make little or no progress despite the provision of personal aids and equipment

- has communication and/or interaction difficulties, and requires specific individual interventions in order to access learning

At this point, staff should consult you as SENCO and together you should try to gather all the information you are able to about the child. You should include observations, assessments, discussions with the child, their parents and any professionals (social services, health visitors, educational psychologists etc).

Early Years Action

You will now need to make sure that the setting and the child's parents co-operate and agree on the action needed to support the child in making progress.

The Code of Practice states that for a child whose needs are to be met through Early Years Action, support could include:

- Extra adult time in devising the nature of the planned intervention and monitoring its effectiveness;

- Providing different learning materials or specific equipment;

- Some individual or group support;

- Staff development and training to introduce more effective strategies.

It may be that you are able to provide this training through your LEA or you may need to seek more specialist advice from relevant organisations or support services.

When a decision has been made on what action will be needed to support the child's progress, it is likely you will consider drawing up an Individual Education Plan (IEP). This is particularly important in recording the strategies you are going to use.

The IEP should contain information on targets set for the child, the teaching strategies and provision to be put in place and a date for review of progress. Details of this progress can then be added at the review.

Early Years Action Plus

It is important to carry out regular reviews of the child's progress with parents and colleagues. If after these reviews you feel the child is still not making progress, you will probably need to seek additional advice from outside agencies. It is also possible that some children may already be at this stage when they join your setting. Even when outside agencies are involved you, as SENCO, will continue to take the leading role, alongside the child's teacher/key worker.

The Code of Practice states that the practitioner who works day to day with the child, and the SENCO, should be given advice and support from outside specialists. Early Years Action Plus is characterised by this involvement and external support services will be able to provide support and advice on target setting, strategies, materials and resources. It is important to research the type of support available within your own LEA/EYDCP and familiarise yourself with relevant contacts.

Referrals to outside agencies

It is your responsibility to make initial contact and forward copies of the records you have collated (with parents' consent). These should include IEPs, reviews, observations and assessments. This will help in establishing what support has already been provided and how.

Using this information and their own observations of the child, they will then be able to offer advice on suitable strategies to use to support the child in working towards these targets. This can then be used when drawing up the child's next IEP. From now on you will have the support of outside agencies in monitoring and reviewing the child's progress.

Individual Education Plans

All children placed on Early Years Action, Early Years Action Plus and those with a statement of special educational needs should have an Individual Education Plan or IEP. An IEP is a working document which enables you to plan individually for children with special educational needs, detailing what is additional to or different from what you usually provide. IEPs should be easy to understand and form an effective working document for everyone who works with the child.

As SENCO, it is your responsibility to oversee the development of IEPs, although you may not be expected to write each one. This will depend on the requirements of your setting but you will certainly be expected to support the child's key worker in setting appropriate targets and strategies.

Confidentiality

Although IEP's contain no 'highly confidential' information they can include personal details about the child's health and in turn are deemed 'sensitive' material under the Data Protection Act 1998. Although they must be shared with everyone working with the child, confidentiality and child protection should be considered - (SEN Code of Practice 4.28/Section 14 SEN Toolkit)

All IEP's should be:

■ treated sensitively

■ not left around

■ stored securely

■ not removed from the setting without the SENCO's permission

■ Shredded when finished with (after required archiving period)

What should an IEP contain?

The major role of the IEP is to set targets for the child. These targets will be decided upon based on a thorough assessment of the child's needs and progress to date. It is important to involve the child, parents, staff and any other professionals working with the child in setting targets that are realistic and achievable.

How should targets be set?

When setting targets, it is worth considering the SMART technique to make sure targets are:

■ Specific

■ Measurable

■ Achievable

■ Relevant

■ Timebound

Targets will vary according to the child's individual needs. For most children, targets will reflect the need to break down tasks into manageable steps. During the Early Years Foundation Stage, it is likely that targets for some children will include aspects of dressing, eating and other areas of personal independence. Remember, however, to make sure that targets are ones you hope the child will achieve within the timescale of the IEP. The teaching strategies to be used and additional provision or resources needed to support the child in achieving set targets will also need to be noted.

Reviewing IEPs

It is important to continually review progress towards targets, with more formal reviews being held per term. The Code of Practice states that IEPs should be reviewed regularly and at least three times a year.

All relevant parties need to be involved in the review process. Parents' views on their child's progress must be sought and they should be consulted when reviewing targets and setting new ones. The child's parents should be asked their opinion and their points considered, if this is difficult the parents can reflect their needs and feelings. If outside professionals are involved, they may not be able to attend every meeting but you can still involve them in the review process by asking for updated information in a written format or through a telephone discussion.

When all this information has been gathered you will be able to consider the progress the child has made and the effectiveness of the IEP and take into account any new information or advice when setting targets for the next IEP. New targets should be set by appropriate staff with the involvement of the child and parent where possible.

There is no set format for IEPs. Your local authority may have their own system and a sample one is provided for you in this book on page 85. You are likely to find that the most effective IEP is one you devise yourself as this will be suited to your setting and the children attending.

Sue Fisher, early years training consultant.

For more on Developing Inclusive Practice see page 5.

SEN Code of Practice: http://www.teachernet.gov.uk/_doc/3724/SENCodeOfPractice.pdf

Sample IEP

Individual education plan

For: Sam Fisher   D.O.B: 10.02.07

(Early Years Action) / Action Plus / Statement of SEN

Period of plan: Summer term   Date: 20.04.10

Strengths / interests	Learning needs
Hand – eye co-ordination – loves jigsaws, Lego, sand. Enjoys investigative play. Good computer skills.	Usually plays alone. Short concentration span in group work/story time.

Targets	Strategies
To play alongside other children. To join a group story session.	Remove obvious distractions. Offer support and praise. Encourage Sam to play in role-play area/areas of co-operative play.

Resources	Monitoring, assessment and success criteria
Role play/dressing up. Sand and water play. Outdoor play house. Additional staff support at story time.	Record weekly observations and monthly updates towards targets. Record in profile.

Agreed by:

_____ SENCO

_____ Parent

Date for review: 20.07.10

Considering early years action plus

What are the concerns about the child?

- Their response to others/the environment or tasks
- Their progress, sensory/communication/developmental issues

Who is expressing them?

- Parents
- Key/family worker
- Nursery worker etc.

What evidence do you have for these concerns?

- Oral/written reports
- Observations
- Progress records
- Medical information

Have you been undertaking and documenting child observations?

- At different times of the day
- In different areas

Are there any known factors that may affect the child's learning/behaviour?

- The setting, people around them, teaching, organisation or preferred ways of learning

Have you consulted with other members of staff and previous carers?

Are you aware of any outside agency involvement?

- Health Visitor
- Speech Therapist
- Psychologist
- Paediatrician etc.

Have you attempted to gain the views of the child? How? When?

Have you consulted with parents? How? When?

What strategies have been used within the planned differentiated curriculum?

Finally, as listed in the Code of Practice, are the interventions needed additional to and different from the setting's differentiated learning opportunities?

NO
Continue meeting child's needs through differentiated approaches/curriculum.

YES
Enter on SEN Register or Early Action.
SENCO to complete the Child Information Record

Prioritise the continuing concerns about the child?

The Code of Practice states to consider Early Action Plus if the child:

- Continues working at levels below that expected of children of a similar age
- Continues to make little or no progress in specific areas
- Has an emotional/behavioural difficulty which interferes with the child's own learning or that of the setting, despite having a behaviour management programme
- Has social issues that hamper the development of relationships and/or cause learning issues
- Has sensory or physical needs which require regular advice, specialist services and additional specialist equipment

What evidence do you have for these concerns?

IEP review:

- Rates of progress observed and assessed
- Targets achieved or not achieved
- Progress not adequate or reasonable
- Parents, child or professionals reporting lack of change/improvement
- Parents, child or professionals concerned with lack of change/improvement
- Medical/social/developmental/physical change in circumstances

What strategies have been used within Early Years Action to address these concerns?

Consider the strategies recorded in IEPs.

- Any one-on-one support?
- Teaching methods
- Differentiation
- Groupings
- Approaches

As well as input from parents and other professionals.

What are the views of the parents?

What are the views of the child?

Has there been any consultation with external services for advice?

Is it agreed that interventions are needed which require the involvement of external support services?

NO
Continue meeting the child's needs through Early Years Action

YES
Early Action Plus/Refer to Multi Agency Team

Selena Ledgerton
Education & Childcare Consultant/Author

Developing your SEN policy

The revised Code of Practice places a requirement on all settings in receipt of Government funding to have a written special educational needs policy and a major part of the SENCO's role is the day-to-day operation of this policy.

You may have inherited an existing policy which will need amending to fulfil the requirements of new legislation or you may need to devise a completely new one. Either way, the policy must promote equal opportunities and the inclusion of children with special educational needs and this is an ideal opportunity to analyse your special needs provision and identify what you really want to do.

Guidance on policy is available in the Code of Practice, from your local authority who will be able to provide details of their policies and procedures and, for non-maintained settings, in the Conditions of Grant.

Staff discussion points
It is important that any policy is understood and followed by all staff members. Involving everyone in its development will help to give a feeling of ownership and increase understanding. Discuss the following with staff to ensure thorough and thoughtful coverage.

The process of developing a policy is as important as the implementation. It offers staff a valuable opportunity to air their views on how they can integrate children with special educational needs.

The policy should reflect the ethos and individuality of your setting and ensure the effectiveness of your practice through inclusion.

What should it contain?
Before planning your policy, familiarise yourself with all relevant documentation, in particular the Code of Practice and *SEN Toolkit*. Non-maintained settings must also include in their policies the information set out in the Conditions of Grant. You can then use the following headings as discussion

points with staff to ensure thorough and thoughtful coverage.

Objectives
Discuss what you are hoping to achieve and how it relates to the Code of Practice. This will help you to draw up clear, concise objectives which should reflect the philosophy of your setting.

Admission arrangements
These should already be in place. What else would you need to consider before admitting a child with special educational needs?

Identification, assessment and provision for all children with special education needs
The sooner special educational needs are identified, the sooner extra support can be provided. You will need to consider who will carry out assessment of need and how. Think about allocation of resources, including human, and ongoing assessment and review of a child's special educational needs.

Access to the full Early Years Foundation Stage curriculum
Consider differentiation and the levels of support available within your setting for children with special educational needs, including such issues as access for disabled children and how you intend to draw up Individual Education Plans, taking into account the guidance in the Code of Practice for Early Years Action and Early Years Action Plus, and for children with statements of special educational needs.

Partnership with parents
Consider how you inform parents of their own and their child's rights, involve them and take into account their own and their child's wishes and ensure they are aware of the local parent partnership services.

Links with other relevant bodies
Your policy should include a brief

description of your arrangements for linking with others on special needs issues, exchanging information as necessary. This should include outside agencies and support services. Consider links with schools and other early years settings and in particular transfer arrangements.

Staff roles and responsibilities
Include brief information on the responsibilities of the SENCO, key workers and other staff members. The name of the SENCO should be in the policy document. Remember to consider arrangements for staff training, in particular SENCO training which should be fed back to the staff team.

You should also look at how you will deal with complaints about your SEN provision, reviewing the policy regularly and addressing problems. These arrangements should take into account the effectiveness of your provision for both individual children and all the children in your setting through assessing the effectiveness of Individual Education Plans, curriculum planning for groups of children and the effectiveness of staff training.

Reviewing your policy
It is a requirement of the Code of Practice that the policy should be regularly monitored, reviewed and evaluated. No policy should be seen as set in stone. It is important to carry out the review arrangements stated in your policy regularly and be prepared to make changes. Putting your policy into practice will highlight any gaps or problems. Remember, a policy is only as good as its implementation.

Sue Fisher,
early years training consultant.

For further information on The role of the SENCO see page 2.

Publications

SEN Code of Practice, DfES 2001
SEN Toolkit, DfES 2001
Requirements of Nursery Education Grant 2001/2 DfEE

The disability discrimination act: how it affects you

Further information on the Disability Discrimination Act can be obtained from the Equality and Human Rights Commission on 0845 604 610 or online at www.equalityhumanrights.com/

Disabled children need and want to play as much as and alongside their non-disabled peers. Yet as a result of social and environmental barriers, many disabled children are missing out on this essential part of growing up.

Play and early years workers are in a position to make a difference, and can begin to lead the way in promoting good practice in inclusive play. Disabled children have a right to play and be included in their local communities. This right is now firmly enshrined in disability legislation.

The Disability Discrimination Act: how it affects you

Disability Discrimination Act (DDA)
The SEN and Disability Act 2001 and the Disability Discrimination Act 2005 amended version of the Disability Discrimination Act 1995.

All settings and local authorities are covered by the DDA.

Early years settings that are not constituted as schools are covered by Part 3 of the Disability Discrimination Act. This requires settings:

■ Not to treat disabled children 'less favourably'. Not to treat pupils who have a disability less favourably, for a reason which relates to their disability, (without justification).

■ To make 'reasonable adjustments' for disabled children. Settings have a responsibility to make 'reasonable adjustments' so that pupils with a disability are not placed at a substantial disadvantage. 'Reasonable adjustments' can mean offering information in different formats, making adjustments to procedures, offering other services, making alterations to the physical features

of buildings or offering an auxiliary service such as a British Sign Language Interpreter.

Please be aware that it is unclear which aspects of disability are covered by the Disability Discrimination Act and when settings MUST make 'reasonable adjustments'. Further clarification has been requested from the Government in their next revision, though it is possible to gain insight from research.

For example:

In July 2009 a school was found to have not made 'reasonable adjustments' for a child with behavioural problems. After the child was excluded following an incident, the school was held accountable under the Disability Discrimination Act for not offering the child support earlier that was available to them - [2009] EWHC 1842 (Admin). With this in mind we can assume that behavioural disorders are included.

There are no requirements on Education Authorities to have an accessibility strategy for early years settings, other than in relation to the schools maintained by them. Equally, there are no requirements on early years settings, other than those constituted as schools, to have a published plan to increase access for young disabled children.

The Disability Discrimination Act 2005 requires settings that are constituted as schools:

■ Not to treat disabled pupils 'less favourably'.

■ To make reasonable adjustments to ensure that disabled pupils are not at a substantial disadvantage.

■ To draw up plans to show how, over time, they will increase access to education for disabled pupils (school accessibility plans).

■ To comply with the Disability Equality Duty.

■ To prepare, publish, implement and report on a Disability Equality Scheme.

Further information on the Disability Discrimination Act, Equality Duty & Equality Scheme can be found here at http://www.teachernet.gov.uk/wholeschool/disability/disabilityandthedda/

What do I need to do?
As well as following the Disability Discrimination Act legislation, here are

a few guidelines that may help when planning. More practical ideas can be found on the following page.

Planning for young disabled children should:

- Concentrate on including the child – there is always a way!

- Consider their emotional and physical wellbeing as well as their 'need'.

- Put the child's learning first and utilise both new & successful strategies.

- Blend well with other provision and providers.

- Build partnerships with parents and carers.

- Take account of the views of those involved.

- Build staff skills and confidence in working with disabled children.

- Build an understanding of the role and responsibilities of different adults in relation to disabled children.

- Be underpinned by a clear vision of how all settings meet their responsibilities to disabled/SEN children.

- Build relationships with other services.

The setting as a whole should:

- Increase access to the curriculum.

- Concentrate on the emotional and physical wellbeing of the child.

- Complete regular risk assessments where required.

- Improve the physical environment to increase access.

- Provide various communication/ access options for disabled children.

- Review strategies and approaches regularly to evaluate how successful they are.

- Address the child as they do everyone else – speak to them directly in a normal tone (not over their head or with pity).

Children are children first and have the right to be treated as such.

Encourage everyone in your setting to include a disabled child by example:

A staff member is assisting Michael to walk outside with toys; Michael is the only child in the class with a disability.

A parent approaches the door and the staff member smiles, "Hi can I help?" The parent just stares at Michael's disability, so the aware staff member adds "This is Michael; it's his turn to help me bring the toys out for the other children today - are you Steven's Mum? He's just inside... (She laughs) It's his turn tomorrow."

Improving Access:

- Identify factors that enable or hinder access for young disabled children – act on them.

- Concentrate on the emotional and physical wellbeing of the child.

- Devise a planned approach to removing barriers that young disabled children face.

- Gain the best possible advantage for young disabled children by combining resources and sharing what works across settings.

- Aim to co-ordinate action with connecting schools and your LEA.

- Link to the Early Support Programme, the Government programme to achieve better co-ordinated family services for young disabled people and their families.

The Early Support Programme is an important part of Every Child Matters.

Further details can be found here: www.dcsf.gov.uk/everychildmatters/ healthandwellbeing/ahdc/ earlysupport/home/

Challenging discrimination - overcoming barriers

Setting up an inclusive play project is not easy. It presents many challenges, and there are many barriers to overcome – not least barriers of attitude and how society views disability. Negative attitudes from parents and carers of non-disabled children is not uncommon. They may be wary about their own children mixing with disabled children or be ambivalent about the idea of inclusion. Then there are the concerns of parents of disabled children who may worry about the level of care their children will receive, the safety of

Celebrating difference and diversity in the classroom

You may want to include some children's books that refer to diversity, disability and disfigurement on the bookshelf. Choose titles that don't isolate those who are different but integrate them.

Include diverse, disabled and disfigured puppets in your puppet box – show that everyone is the same even though they are different. Puppets are available with birthmarks, wheelchairs and missing limbs to name but a few.

Why would they not be included? Children learn discriminatory tendencies – there are bookable puppet shows available that use disabled or disfigured puppets to encourage children to see each other as children first.

When the children watch TV or a film, select something regularly that subtly includes diversity, disfigurements and disabilities. The piece should be age-appropriate and differences should not be pointed out. You are making the sub-conscious suggestion that differences don't make you different – we are all the same valuable human beings. Can't think of something? How about Disney's *Finding Nemo* to start you off? Nemo has a malformed fin, Gill a facial disfigurement and the underwater world is very diverse.

the environment, and the reactions of other children.

Most of these attitudes arise from fear and ignorance, and it is only through challenging discrimination and awareness raising with parents that we will begin to change attitudes. As for the children, the most common reaction to difference is one of curiosity and acceptance - particularly in the early years. Let's capitalise on this and start the process of moving towards a society where all children, regardless of disability, ethnicity or any other difference, can play together in a supportive environment without fear of prejudice or discrimination.

Rachel Scott,
Policy and Publications Officer, Kidsactive.

Observation record

Child's name	Date

Focus/purpose of observation

Details of observation/behaviours, learning difficulties observed

Evaluation/suggestions

Signed _____

Expression of concern

Child's name	Date

What difficulties are evident?

What strategies have been tried in response to these needs?

Which outside agencies have been consulted/with what outcomes?

Signed _____

Individual education plan

For: D.O.B:

Early Years Action / Action Plus / Statement of SEN

Period of plan: Date:

Strengths / interests	Learning needs

Targets	Strategies

Resources	Monitoring, assessment and success criteria

Agreed by:

_____ SENCO

_____ Parent

Date for review:

Review document

Child's name	Date

Progress made towards targets

Effectiveness of strategies/plan

Parental support/external agencies

New/updated information

Future action

Present at review

Signed _____

Useful contacts

- *Special Educational Needs a Guide for Parents & Carers* has now been fully revised (2009) and is available from the Department for Schools and Families Website: www.teachernet.gov. uk/docbank/index.cfm?id=3755

- All SEN Publications from the Department for Schools and Families Website: www.teachernet.gov. uk/wholeschool/sen/publications/ index.cfm

- **Department for Education**
  Sanctuary Buildings, Great Smith Street, London, SW1P 3BT
  Tel: 0870 000 2288
  Email: info@dcsf.gsi.gov.uk
  www.dcsf.gov.uk

- **Every Child Matters**
  Tel: 087 0000 2288
  Website: www.dcsf.gov.uk/ everychildmatters/earlyyears/ familyinformationservice

- **Every Child Matters Family Information Service**
  Website: www.dcsf.gov.uk/ everychildmatters/earlyyears/ familyinformationservice
  Tel: 087 0000 2288

- **ADDISS - ADHD Information Service**
  PO Box 340, Edgware, Middlesex, HA8 9HL
  Tel: 020 8952 2800
  Email: info@addiss.co.uk
  Website: www.addiss.co.uk/
  ADDISS also have a resource centre and reference library (contacts available on site)

- **Action for Leisure**
  Warwickshire College, Moreton Morrell, Warwickshire CV35 7PP
  Tel: 01926 650195
  Website: www.inclusive.co.uk/ support/actleisure.shtml

- **Advisory Centre for Education (ACE)**
  1C Aberdeen Studios,
  22 Highbury Grove, London N5 2DQ
  General Advice Line: 0808 800 5793
  Website: www.ace-ed.org.uk
  A national advice centre for parents

offering information and support about state education in England and Wales for five- to 16-year-olds.

- **Afasic Unlocking Speech and Language**
  1st Floor, 20 Bowling Green Lane, London, EC1R 0BD
  Tel (administration): 020 7490 9410
  Afasic Helpline:0845 3 55 55 77
  Website: www.afasic.org.uk
  The UK charity representing children and young adults with communication impairments.

- **Association of Speech and Language Therapists (ASLTIP)**
  Coleheath Bottom, Speen, Princes Risborough, Bucks, HP27 0SZ
  Tel: 01494 488306
  Website: www.helpwithtalking.com

- **Brain Gym**
  12 Golders Rise, Hendon, London, NW4 2HR
  Tel: 0845 539 0312
  Website: www.braingym.org.uk

- **British Dyslexia Association**
  Unit 8, Bracknell Beeches, Old Bracknell Lane, Bracknell, RG12 7BW
  Tel: 0845 251 9003
  National Helpline: 0845 251 9002
  Website: www.bdadyslexia.org.uk

- **British Stammering Association**
  15 Old Ford Road, London, E2 9PJ
  Helpline - 0845 603 2001
  Website: www.stammering.org

- **Centre for Accessible Environments**
  70 South Lambeth Road, Vauxhall, London, SW8 1RL
  Tel: 020 7840 0125
  Webiste: www.cae.org.uk
  Information access and design.

- **Centre for Studies on Inclusive Education**
  New Redland Building, Coldharbour Lane, Frenchay, Bristol, BS16 1QU
  Tel: 0117 328 4007
  Website: www.csie.org.uk

- **Contact a Family (CAF)**
  209-211 City Road, London, EC1V 1JN
  Tel: 020 7608 8700
  Helpline: 0808 808 3555
  Website: www.cafamily.org.uk
  Provides support and advice to parents of children with special needs.

- **Council for Disabled Children**
  8 Wakley Street, London EC1V 7QE
  Tel: 020 7843 6061
  Email: cdc@ncb.org.uk
  Website: www.ncb.org.uk/cdc.htm

- **Disability Discrimination Act Equality and Human Rights Commission**
  Tel: 0845 604 610
  Website: www.equalityhumanrights.com

- **DIAL UK (Disablement Information and Advice Lines)**
  St Catherines, Tickhill Road, Doncaster, DN4 8QN
  Tel: 01302 310123
  Supports a network of local disablement information and advice officers.

- **Disabled Living Foundation**
  380-384 Harrow Road, London, W9 2HU
  Tel: 0207 289 6111
  Helpline: 0845 130 9177
  Website: www.dlf.org.uk

- **Down's Syndrome Association**
  The Langdon Down Centre,
  2A Langdon Park, Teddington,
  Middlesex, TW11 9PS
  Helpline/Telephone: 0845 230 0372
  Website: www.downs-syndrome.org.uk

- **Dyscovery Centre
  (Dyspraxia & Other Disorders)**
  Allt-Yr-Yn-Campus, University of Wales,
  Newport, NP20 5DA
  Tel: 01633 432 330
  Website: dyscovery.newport.ac.uk
  The centre assesses and treats
  children with dyspraxia but can also
  help with information.

- **Home-Start UK**
  8-10 West Walk, L
  eicester, LE1 7NA
  Tel: 0800 068 63 68
  Website: www.home-start.org.uk

- **Kidsactive (formerly HAPA)**
  Pryor's Bank, Bishop's Park,
  London, SW6 3LA
  Tel: 0207 731 1435 and 020 7736 4443
  National charity providing information
  and training on inclusive play.

- **LOOK Part of the National
  Federation of Families with Visually
  Impaired Children**
  Queen Alexandra College,
  49 Court Oak Road, Harborne,
  Birmingham, B17 9TG.
  Tel: 0121 428 5038
  Website: www.look-uk.org

- **MENCAP**
  123 Golden Lane, London, EC1Y ORT
  Website: www.mencap.org.uk
  Tel: 020 7454 0454
  Can advise on working with children
  with learning difficulties.

- **NAGC
  For Gifted Children and their Families**
  Suite 14 Challenge House, Sherwood
  Drive, Bletchley, Milton Keynes,
  Buckinghamshire, MK3 6DP
  Tel: 0845 450 0295
  Website: www.nagcbritain.org.uk

- **National Association for Special
  Educational Needs (NASEN)**
  NASEN House, 4/5 Amber Business
  Village, Amber Close, Amington,
  Tamworth, B77 4RP
  Tel: 01827 311500
  Website: www.nasen.org.uk

- **National Autistic Society (NAS)**
  393 City Road, London, EC1V 1NG
  Tel: 020 7833 2299
  Helpline: 0845 070 4004

- **National Deaf Children's Society**
  15 Dufferin Street, London, EC1Y 8PD
  Tel: 020 7490 8656
  Minicom: 020 7490 8656
  Website: www.ndcs.org.uk
  Can advise on communicating with
  deaf children.

- **National Portage Association**
  Kings Court, 17 School Road,
  Hall Green, Birmingham, B28 8JG
  Email: info@portage.org.uk
  Website: www.portage.org.uk

- **Obsessive Compulsive Disorder UK**
  PO Box 8955,
  Nottingham, NG10 9AU
  Tel: 0845 120 3778 (Admin)
  Website: www.ocduk.org
  or www.ocdkids.org

- **Parents for Inclusion**
  336 Brixton Road, London, SW9 7AA
  Tel: 020 7738 3888
  Freephone Helpline: 0800 652 3145
  Website: www.parentsforinclusion.org
  An organisation set up by parents of
  disabled children to provide support
  and advice to parents and to campaign
  for the inclusion of disabled children
  in mainstream education.

- **Play Therapy United Kingdom**
  The Coach House, Belmont Road,
  Uckfield, East Sussex, TN22 1BP
  Tel: 01825 761143
  Website: www.playtherapy.org.uk

- **Relax Schools & Relax Kids**
  Website: www.relaxschools.co.uk/
  library.aspx?category=top-tips

- **Royal College of Speech
  and Language Therapists**
  2-3 White Hart Yard,
  London, SE1 1NX
  Tel: 020 7378 1200

- **Royal National Institute for the Blind
  (RNIB)**
  105 Judd Street, London, WC1H 9NE
  Tel: 0207 388 1266
  Website: www.rnib.org.uk
  Can advise on many aspects of play and
  leisure for visually impaired children

- **Scope**
  6 Market Road, London, N7 9PW
  Helpline: 0808 800 3333
  Provides support for children with
  cerebral palsy and related disabilities,
  their parents and carers.

- **The British Association of Art Therapists**
  24-27 White Lion Street,
  London, N1 9PD
  A Company Limited by Guarantee
  No. 01326920 (England & Wales)
  Tel: 020 7686 4216
  Website: www.baat.org

- **The Dyspraxia Foundation**
  8 West Alley, Hitchin, Herts SG5 1EG.
  Tel: 01462 454986
  Website:
  www.dyspraxiafoundation.org.uk

- **The Partially Sighted Society**
  7/9 Bennetthorpe,
  Doncaster, DN2 6AA
  Tel: 0844 477 4966
  Website: www.partsight.org.uk

- **The Speech, Language
  and Hearing Centre**
  Website: www.speech-lang.org.uk

- **Tourettes Action UK**
  Southbank House,
  Black Prince Road, London, SE1 7SJ
  Tel: 0845 458 1252
  Website: www.tourettes-action.org.uk